This Book may be kept

## FOURTEEN DAYS

A fine of TWO CENTS will be charged for each day
the Book is kept over time.

|  |  |  |  |
|---|---|---|---|
|  |  |  |  |
|  |  |  |  |
|  |  |  |  |
|  |  |  |  |
|  |  |  |  |
|  |  |  |  |
|  |  |  |  |
|  |  |  |  |
|  |  |  |  |
|  |  |  |  |
|  |  |  |  |
|  |  |  |  |
|  |  |  |  |
|  |  |  |  |
|  |  |  |  |
|  |  |  |  |
|  |  |  |  |
|  |  |  |  |

# DAYS OF THE PHOENIX

VAN WYCK BROOKS *has written:*

Published by E. P. DUTTON & CO., INC.

# VAN WYCK BROOKS

Bronze Medallion, 1923

by Theodore Spicer-Simson

# DAYS OF
# THE PHOENIX

*The Nineteen-Twenties I Remember*

By Van Wyck Brooks

E. P. DUTTON & COMPANY, INC.

NEW YORK, 1957

## NOTE

THE PAGES THAT FOLLOW are a continuation of my *Scenes and Portraits: Memories of Childhood and Youth*. They take up the story of my life, work and friendships from the year when I settled in Connecticut. Of the six years since I had returned from Europe at the beginning of the first world war, I had spent three in New York, two in California and one in the Wall Street suburb of my childhood.

In gathering together my memories of the nineteen-hundreds, I have had in mind a remark of W. B. Yeats. Urging his father, J. B. Yeats, to tell the story of his life, the poet said, "It would tell people about those things that are not old enough to be in the histories or new enough to be in the reader's mind, and those things are always the things that are least known."

# CONTENTS

DAYS OF THE PHOENIX

## CHAPTER I

## CONNECTICUT: 1920

IN THE years that followed the first world war the quiet Connecticut countryside attracted many of the New York writers
and artists, for the low rolling hills there seemed to favour
those who cared more for the state of their minds than the
state of their fortunes. They were drawn to the pretty villages
and the old farmhouses that were built by faithful craftsmen
a century before,—two centuries in many cases, or nearly three,
—master-carpenters working in a fine tradition, following Pal-
ladian manuals of the colonial time. In the woodland clearings, on the slopes, there were natural pictures on every side
that brought back Giorgione or perhaps Cézanne, and the antique dealers from the city raided the region for the lowboys
they found on lonely roads. The villagers, who had often been
swindled, occasionally cherished as antiques even the stuffed
owls that also abounded in their houses,—they thought any old
book might be a rare first edition; but one still found in 1920
serviceable tables and settees that had been made there in the
sixteen-hundreds. These, with chests of oak and pine, were
emblems of a country that could no longer be called new or
young, for they had been shaped and put together in the
winding lanes there when Molière was living in France and
Milton in England.

This note of the native Connecticut air meant much to the newcomers who were settling in abandoned farmhouses and remodelling barns, aside from the tranquillity one found there in a war-torn world and the charm of old hand-hewn beams and drooping elms. For in many cases the artists and writers had grown up in a still raw West or had returned from Paris in search of "roots," that shy and impalpable quiddity the lack of which, they felt, had made them frequently shallow and generally restless. No word was more constantly on their lips unless it was the native "soil" or "earth," and this obsession lay deep in the minds of urban cosmopolitans whom one saw toiling now with spade and pick. Some of them flew back and forth between their farms and Hollywood, alternating weeks in the studio with weeks in the field, and one found fashion-designers digging rocks out of streams and laboriously piling them up for a dam and a pool. They lovingly pointed out to friends the iron H-hinges on their doors, the twelve-inch planks on their floors and their cavern-like cellars, and they measured the immense cut stones in border walls along which three men could walk abreast. They seemed to draw a secret strength from the old Yankee farmers who had occupied and tilled the land before them, and one met occasionally a survivor on the road who could still speak of the customs and laws of the past. He might answer off-hand, if one asked him what was wrong with some pseudo-colonial house that had just been erected, "The ridge-pole's too high by fourteen inches." In this paradoxical decade, equally full of despair and hope, there were many who flouted tradition and many who sought it, and it was reassuring for these to live in a long settled region. They found at least a rill of tradition there.

No European could understand this constant American talk of roots, or why it was that expatriates discussed expatriation,

—a word that scarcely existed in any other country,—wondering about their "responsibilities" when they were abroad and how long they could safely stay in Europe. Sinclair Lewis told me later that he had read one of my books to find his roots in Connecticut before he moved there, for he had been racketing round the world for the last half-century and felt he had to belong somewhere at last. He had returned to Minnesota, but the world he had known as a child had gone and he could not live with the new people; then he remembered that all his forbears had come from Connecticut and he had returned to this old home of the Yankees. It was true that he did not stay there long, but the question of expatriation was never out of Sinclair Lewis's mind; and it was against the dangers of this that the painter Robert Henri had warned the young dancer Angna Enters. "So many artists go abroad," he had said to her, "and something happens to their work. You must never let that happen to you." But this was natural, surely, if there was any truth in certain comments of other Europeans, that America was "not a blood-homeland," as D. H. Lawrence said, or that Americans were "not yet at home in their unconscious." (This was Dr. Carl Jung's diagnosis.) For me this question was still acute when, in 1920, my wife and I bought a village house in Westport, for I was colonially minded then and was perhaps to remain so, owing to certain elements of my youth and education. It took me twenty years or more to live down what I felt then, a frequently acute homesickness for the European scene, for I had experienced all too fully the widely shared consciousness of a drop in one's emotional thermometer on returning from Europe. It was like the change, for a swimmer, from salt water to fresh. I understood why it was that Thoreau had refused to go abroad, fearing to lose the feeling of his "native woods and pastures," for Americans were so often overborne in Europe. A long immersion in American life was to cure me completely of any lingering fears of expatriation; but this ambivalence characterized my outlook in the twenties, as I was to realize later, looking back.

Westport still had a rustic air, with a wooden hotel on the post-road; and often, on one of the rocking-chairs that lined the long piazza, one saw Bill Hart surrounded with his cronies. The famous and opulent cowboy, the hero of the Westerns, had scarcely emerged from the chrysalis of the old-time actor, but, still a tiro at mounting a horse, he dazzled all the little boys with his trick of lighting a match by flicking a thumbnail. William S. Hart, with his feet on the rail and a ten-gallon hat on the back of his head, recalled a simpler world in the so-called jazz age, while in some of the plain little houses that lined the village streets one found surprising variations of Yankee types. There might have been the scholar I was to know in after years who came "south" for the winter from his village in Vermont, just as the Orkney islanders, to warm their bones in January, descend for a touch of the tropics to Edinburgh. This was the philosophic soul who learned Chinese at seventy-five and who was studying Sanskrit when I knew him at eighty. Our own introduction to the town had been a drive with a friend who took us out to dinner at his solitary farmhouse, showing us, as we sped past, a house where a woman had hanged herself and another where a Swedish officer had murdered his wife. Then, at a turn of the road, a woman in black was bending over, gathering dandelions, and my friend said she was old Kate who had killed her father with a bread-knife and had just been released from the asylum. I had only begun to take it in that all towns were Spoon Rivers and that Edgar Lee Masters had shocked the country merely by showing what one should have known; but

I had found and was to find too many other sorts of life ever to believe in the general depravity of men.

The cottage in which my wife and I were to live for twenty years stood on the old post-road that was called King's Highway. It was perched on a high, rocky, woodsy corner, and the poetess who had lived there and built a tree-house overhead had painted the rooms in the new Greenwich Village fashion. One was canary yellow, another pale apple-green; others were Chinese blue and terracotta. In front a row of Lombardy poplars dropped their golden leaves over the stone wall that shut us in, and we constructed a terrace on the slope over the garden with a table under the shade of an old apple-tree. It was a true *Künstlerheim,* as one of our friends called it, one of the many in whose talk, as we sat under the branches, I felt the time-spirit prompting me.

No one can ever be fully aware of what a given decade means, or whether it is a "period" or an "epoch," as Charles Péguy put it, he who found himself in a tame and pallid 1898 when he longed for a fierce and heroic 1793. But thirty years later, in literary circles, the decade of the twenties was to look rather like an epoch in the minds of the young, at least when they compared it with the decades that followed; and indeed, in those days that were thought of as a little Renaissance, there was much afoot in the world of writers. American writing itself had come to seem important, although it was still ignored in academic circles, where Thackeray and Tennyson were treated as twin kings of our literature and all the American writers as poor relations. It was regarded as "a pale and obedient provincial cousin about which the less said the better," in the phrase of Ernest Boyd, and Christian Gauss at Princeton, as Edmund Wilson soon pointed out, chimed in with Woodberry at Columbia and Wendell at Harvard. He too looked down his nose at American studies. But the idea that America was a dependency of England had vanished, with the world war, from the minds of writers, who were now inclined to agree with Melville that the time had come for America "to set, not follow precedents." They were acutely aware of the country, its promise and its weaknesses, and the problems of the writer living in it, and they were concerned especially with the art of writing.

These questions interested all our friends as we sat under the apple-tree, and it was largely true that American writing had come of age, along with other aspects of the life of the country. This was a time of transition between the colonial or provincial past and the world-minded America of later decades, a time when, in spite of the war that destroyed in Europe so many hopes, this country seemed to be starting, artistically, afresh. A friend of mine in London wrote that England was "a mere standing pool" whereas our American criticism was "living," because in England critics felt that nothing remained to be done while we had "an end for America" and were "working towards it." So, too, at about this time an English traveller noted that literature in England was "in a blind alley" and that we had "the growing end of English literature today" because we had "a new hope with a new impulse." Of this, in fact, there were many examples in the sudden appearance of new good writers and of little theatres and little magazines, with *The Dial, The Masses, The Freeman, The Seven Arts* and *The New Republic,* the New School for Social Research and the Whitney Museum. Most of these institutions rose within a dozen years, following *The Smart Set* of Mencken and the emergence of the "Eight," which marked, with the Armory Show, a new moment in painting, and one might add the Theatre Guild and the discovery of American folk art as notes in this American Risorgimento. (To use the word that Ezra Pound preferred to the commoner American Renaissance.) People were talking *ad libitum* about the "American experience," the "American language," the "American rhythm" and what not, and Vachel Lindsay had announced a great "flowering of art and song," a "spiritual harvest" appearing in the Middle West. There Masters and Sandburg, Eliot and Pound, Sherwood Anderson and Sinclair Lewis were soon to be followed by Hemingway, Dos Passos and Fitzgerald, and Willa Cather was to show in her novels and stories the general aesthetic resources of that multiracial region. In her work one saw the dawning talents of the new immigrant strains that blossomed in prairie villages and bleak ranch-houses, singers like Cressida Garnett, Hungarian violinists and German pianists from Western mining towns. These were among the characters one met in Greenwich Village.

Sooner or later, as an outpost of New York, Westport was to witness many of the types of this time of discovery and youth; for there came Sherwood Anderson and Scott Fitzgerald, along with the New England poet Robert Frost. There, too, lived Paul Rosenfeld, of all our Westport circle of friends the most aware, I think, of the promise of the country, alive as he was to music and painting as well as to literature and an absolute worshipper of art. "To have artists about one is wonderful," he wrote in a letter, "and to be loved by them almost divine," and no one recognized and hailed so many of the new talents from Georgia O'Keeffe, the painter, to Marianne Moore. When he built a cottage not far from ours, he employed to paint it not two house-painters but two "art-artists,"—in the phrase of a politician much quoted at the time,—members of the circle of Alfred Stieglitz, who was Paul's elder cousin and to whom he looked up as a prophet and almost a father. As I passed the house on afternoon walks I saw the two sitting on the roof, in the sunny May weather, discussing art, and they were there for many weeks, occasionally taking a moment off to fill their brushes for a few strokes of paint. But Paul, who had ample means, never thought of hastening them, for helping impecunious artists was one of his chief pleasures: it was, in fact, his way of offering thanks to the artist-clan who made the world luminous and habitable for himself and others. "I wish I might do something to make your life and everybody's life in the U.S.A. more fruitful," Paul wrote to one of our friends. "I should like to be able to fight for you and all the rest who are doing good work, and create some sort of atmosphere in which it is easier for such as you to exist." He had mourned over the young musicians who were killed or wounded in the war and the painters who were starving to death in Russia, and he was beloved in turn as a true-born citizen of the fatherland of art who scarcely admitted any other allegiance.

Art for Paul could be only "pure." It had no connection with history, economics, society or any alloy, and artists for him were sacrosanct, moreover. He thought of it as treason if, in any fashion, one challenged their claims; and, generous as he was to me, he looked at me askance when I published *The Ordeal of Mark Twain*. There, from his point of view, I had committed two sins, "attacking" a writer, in the first place, and, secondly, regarding him from the social, not the aesthetic, point of view. He felt I was handing a writer over to the secular arm of the Philistines and, in so doing, betraying my own caste; and he excommunicated Carl Sandburg a little later after praising him also highly in *Port of New York*. He had rejoiced in the "wonder and song" that Carl Sandburg had found in his Western towns, in the Mississippi valley that he

saw as the top of the globe, saying that Sandburg had virtually done for the Western townspeople what Synge had
done for the language of the Irish peasants. I had first met
Sandburg in Paul's own rooms in town, but, for him, this
poet had committed an act of treason that was even graver
than my own, for he had written a book in praise of Edward
Steichen, his brother-in-law and an old associate of Stieglitz.
The trouble was that Steichen had broken the unwritten code
of artists by using his photographs in advertising; and how
could one pardon anyone for defending such a man? This was
a sin that Paul could see only as mortal. Nor could he endure
bleak thinking in criticism. He referred to the "sad disgruntled beings" who wrote *Civilization in the United States* and
who complained that the American soil was unfriendly to the
growth of art when there was John Marin, for one, blooming
and singing. Did not Marin, all ebullience and high spirit,
suggest a fruit-tree rooted in good ground?

Like Huneker, who said he had always rejoiced when he
caught the first glow of a rising sun, Paul too was a yea-sayer
who had much in common with this earlier star-finder of the
various arts. But while Huneker had discovered, for America,
European talents, Paul found these talents at home, and few
of his swans turned out to be geese, for he saw in his own
time what others were to see twenty years later. There had
been a day for him when any German village, or any garden
in Holland or balcony in France, had stirred him as New
York had never done, but another day came when the port,
as the steamer approached it, had filled him with a sense of
confidence and strength. He had found himself entering a
country where, as he said, it was "good to be," where a new
spirit was obviously dawning, and, if "every generation," as

John Sloan said, "is *the* generation to an artist," no one was more aware than Paul of this one.

It was true that in painting Paul scarcely strayed beyond the borders of Stieglitz's group,—he could not in his heart believe in a painter who did not have the Stieglitz *imprimatur*; but in literature and music,—his special field in criticism, —he was adventurous and prophetic at the same time. In his musical chronicle in *The Dial* he saluted Carl Ruggles and Ernest Bloch and said "Roger Sessions goes to a great career," for he found in American music, at last, the robustness and the vibrancy that had been generally lacking in the older composers. In literature too he was one of the first to acclaim the new novelists and poets who were beginning to appear in the early twenties, among them E. E. Cummings and Wallace Stevens. A true apostle of all art, Paul would appear from time to time with a picture of Marsden Hartley's under his arm, or one by our fellow-Westporter Arthur Dove which he called "a sort of *Leaves of Grass* through pigment," covering our dining-room walls with them for a few weeks or months so that the new sun would also dawn for us. He was all for what he called "the dream growing out of reality," which he welcomed in Marin, Dove and Hartley, while he turned away from the bloodless dream of Arthur B. Davies, for instance, that left reality itself wingless and shoddy.

Nothing could have been more remote than Paul's impressionistic style from the stripped prose that soon became the vogue, one all romantic luxuriance and sometimes rhapsodic, the other analytic, spare and cold. Paul, as a man of feeling, was to find himself less and less at home in a world of cerebration and specialization, while he brought his readers what later critics scarcely wished to bring them, the glamour of a literary life that seemed all enjoyment. Some of the essays in his *Musical Portraits* were among the finest of their time, those, for example, on César Franck, on Berlioz, on Moussorgsky and on Wagner as a symbol of his epoch and Debussy of ours (or, one should say, of the period when this essay was written). For the rest, it was Paul's misfortune that he wrote occasionally as if English was not his native language. He had grown up in a music-loving German-Jewish family with early associations that were Central European, and his writing abounded in preciosities, neologisms and archaisms that one seldom found in the work of born writers of English. Paul's exceptional gift of style made it all the plainer that he was not quite at home in the language he wrote in, and all this told against him in the minds of later writers who had none of his cultivation and little of his talent. But there were many of all schools who felt they were indebted to him, as critic, editor or friend, for their public existence, and no one deserved more the epithet of Emerson,—he was a consistent "patriot of the muses' country."

Paul had been our first Westport guest, in 1920, in the garden. He had joined us at a nursery lunch with rice pudding and the children. Meanwhile, either at his house or at Karl Anderson's near the beach, Sherwood Anderson appeared for an occasional visit, and, although these were his roaming years in the mid-America that he called "my land," he even thought for a while of living near us. I had first known him earlier, and he sometimes wrote to me from the strange places where he liked to be alone, wandering with what he described as "mystic vague impulses," but with a clear eye also, from town to town. He would disappear for months, no one knew where he was, or he would set out on a walking trip across Illinois in ploughing time; and he wrote once from Reno that he felt "people by thousands" somehow "drifting in and out of me."

His actual physical feeling of being completely in rapport with every man, woman and child along the street had become so intense one afternoon that he felt obliged to "hide" himself to rest. From the time when, as a little boy, he had tagged at the heels of older men, listening to their talk, observing their quirks, working himself in the fields with them or tending horses at county fairs, he had been aware of all sorts and conditions of men. But he was especially drawn to the human grotesques and the obscure of whom he wrote, "It is they who have given me life." For he shared the preference of the "little people" over the "big" so generally shown in novels of the two world wars, in which the officers are never as good as the men; and I remember that at Westport once he burst out about Robert E. Lee, against whom he seemed to have a special grudge. He said he was going to write a book about the Civil War that would put these stuffed shirts in their places. To this degree Sherwood carried the cult of the rank and file, the magnet of the American imagination.

Aside from his people, Sherwood's mind was alive with images of the West. He wrote to me, for instance, about *Poor White,* the story of a "Lincolnian type from Missouri," that the book was "about laid by, as we say out here of the corn crop in early October. It is in shocks and stood up in the field. The husking is yet to do." But he kept repeating, "It's lonely out here" and "We are all struggling in a vacuum . . . One gets this queer sense of carving a stone that will be cast into a stagnant sea, into the Sargasso sea, as you suggest" (in my book *America's Coming-of-Age*). This loneliness, which we all felt, drew him into the Stieglitz circle, and there, and still more later, in the circle of Gertrude Stein, he began to worry about "sophistication." In Stieglitz, loving his tools and materials, Sherwood saw the craftsman whom he admired above all other types, a symbol of the old wagon-builders, organ-builders and harness-makers who had been swept away by the factory system. But in the Stieglitz atmosphere there was another element that spoiled his natural simplicity a little, for it made him feel that he should follow what he called "European moods" instead of the "old mood" of his early stories. Luckily, he could return at times to this old mood that belonged to him, and how good it was to hear him talk about "Buck Fever" and "Hannah Stoots" in his newspaper days in Virginia later. But in much of his work he became artificially simple, with a naivety that seemed both forced and knowing. It was this that Hemingway took for affectation when he travestied Sherwood Anderson in *The Torrents of Spring*.

Sherwood's two brothers in Westport were troubled by this trait of his, or, I should say, the mendacity it sometimes led to, the conscious use of fantasy in dealing with fact. Of these two, Karl, the painter, was altogether without guile, and Ray was all too genuinely simple. This maverick, a much younger man, could not stomach Sherwood's "lies," insisting that their grandmother was Italian, for example, when everybody knew that she was German; and in fact Sherwood's non-fictional writing would have been far more interesting if he had not strayed over the fictional border. But in all this drawing of the long bow he was following the father whom he described in the character of Windy McPherson and from whom he had inherited the gift of story-telling that seemed in all three brothers exactly the same. When Ray stopped me on the street to tell me how, when he was a boy, he had caught mud-turtles in Ohio, I could not believe it was not Sherwood speaking, and when I read a novel once that Karl took it into his head to write I felt that Sherwood must have written this novel.

The voices of all three brothers were as much alike as the themes and the style of their stories.

With John Held, who created it partly in his drawings and his stories, the note of the jazz age also resounded in Westport, where Scott Fitzgerald, who presently spent a summer there, summoned the fire department during one wild party. He was ready when the firemen came with an explanation that not his house but he and his friends were "lit." After another party a young man whom we all knew laid himself down on the post-road to be run over by a truck. This was the day of the bootlegger and the "liberated love-making" of Edmund Wilson's *Memoirs of Hecate County*, tales of the princess with golden hair and the shooter of snapping-turtles who lived, if not in Westport, certainly near us. As one of a younger generation,—we had a new generation every five years, Stieglitz said,—Wilson visited Paul in the early twenties, and later I wondered if Paul had not suggested to him the art-critic who appeared as the fictional narrator in this book of stories. Near us lived Guy Pène du Bois, and Everett Shinn, one of the "Eight," bought a big house on the post-road surrounded by a wall where he was writing novels and plays to work off some of the energy that his painting seemed unable to exhaust. One night at our house he acted out a whole play for us, and the fiery wiry little man sprang about our living-room, now speaking in the voice of one character, now of another. A few doors from us was the novelist William McFee, the retired ship's engineer who had grown up in England. He had sailed with coal from Cardiff to the Canary Islands, with kerosene to Yokohama, with cotton from Charleston, to Singapore, Surabaya and Rio de Janeiro, and, after writing *Casuals of the Sea* during a brief visit home, he was at work on *Harbours of Memory* in Westport. There, off and on, were the Prender-

gasts, Maurice and the younger Charles, who lived there always after his brother's death,—the master-craftsman who
knew so well the superlative wood-carving of Italy and Spain
and who framed so many of Mrs. Jack Gardner's pictures. It
was during these years that he developed, in his gilded images
and gesso panels, an art of happy visions, all his own, with
flashing fountains, windblown girls and the fairy-tale animals
and ships of a personal Yankee golden age and world.

In Westport lived the grocer who struck a key-note of the
time, as it comes back to me in a very different epoch,—a picturesque man who had once been a trader in the jungle of
South Africa and who let his accounts with artists run for
years. One day he showed me a postal order he had just received from Bali settling the bill of a painter that was ten
years old, and his comment was that in all his experience he
had never had a bad debt that concerned a man of the brush
or a man of the pen. I was all the more impressed by this because two Westport tradesmen could not be induced to send
me bills at all and I had to wait three years, in one case, in
the other nine, before I knew what I had spent over their
counters. They looked on outstanding bills as money in the
bank, one of them said, and it was evident that long experience had justified this virtually instinctive faith in men. I
wondered at the time if New England was peculiarly honest.
But I think Sherwood Anderson's trust in man's essential de-
cency was generally characteristic of the mind of the country.
It was certainly characteristic of most of the writers, who still
saw man as basically good, indefinitely plastic and capable of
introducing a new order in the world. If, thirty-five years
later, "A good man is hard to find" might have been taken as
their motto, this was an after-effect of war on a younger generation that "likes to believe the worst of everybody." (A

phrase of John Peale Bishop in one of his essays.) It was a delayed reaction, in the jargon of psychology, and one that was rather slow in coming on, for the writers of the twenties still widely shared the faith of the Enlightenment in human perfectibility and good will. The Utopian hope that had few roots in Europe had lingered from colony times in the American mind.

## CHAPTER II

# THE NEWNESS

I HAD FIRST met Sherwood Anderson in 1917, three years before I moved to Westport, in the rooms of the monthly *The
Seven Arts,* which expressed what the editor called a sense of
"the brighter colour of a new day." James Oppenheim had
written *Songs for the New Age,* Whitmanesque poems that
conveyed this feeling of promise at a time when dozens of
novelists and poets were "discovering" America and a spirit
of rebirth was in the air. "It is our faith and the faith of many
that we are living in the first days of a renascent period . . .
the beginning of greatness," Waldo Frank had written in a
manifesto that appeared in the first number of the magazine.
As I recall it, Waldo Frank was the real creator of *The Seven
Arts,* and, as associate editor, he had procured for this the first
of Sherwood Anderson's *Winesburg* stories. I was invited to
join the staff because my *America's Coming-of-Age* had also
struck the note of the new day.

Ever since I had come home from Europe at the outset of
the war, I had been working in a New York publishing office,
in the Century Company where one saw, drifting in and out,
the gentlemanly old-fashioned authors of the "Howells and
James" age. Howells himself might have been there, the last
of the triumvirate who had survived Mark Twain and Henry
James and whom I had interviewed some years before, the

novelist of a domestic world in which silver weddings and bridal tours, together with the servant problem, filled people's minds. Howells, who had also survived his vogue, stood for an Anglo-American past that seemed now almost as remote as the past of Persia, a day when American writing itself had been taken lightly and every eye but Howells's was turned towards England. But other kindly old men of letters, often wearing beards, dropped in, uniting the Century Company with the Century Club, where with one voice they denounced the new novelists and poets who were equally outlandish in their literary manners and their names. Moreover, they denounced Amy Lowell, who was putting the new poetry on the map with a species of bad manners that belied her name and whom I first saw in the office of *The Century* as, one day, I passed the editor's door. There I observed a bright green expanse, broad as a meadow in springtime,—Amy Lowell's back, —which blocked the door, while her commanding voice rang down the hallway. Like Robert Frost, John Dos Passos and Theodore Dreiser, she too was one of the writers of *The Seven Arts.*

Meanwhile, at the Century Company, I had been busy for many weeks ghost-writing the memoirs of Iliodor, the "mad monk of Russia," who came to the office every day and poured out, through an interpreter, the story that I was to organize into a book. Odorous and fat as a porpoise, this greatest of Russian church orators brought back the mediæval Slavic folk-world, the moujik world of the Slavophiles who wished to preserve the old Russia from what they regarded as the devilish spirit of the West. With fanatical zeal he had defended autocracy and orthodoxy, an idol of the masses and a preacher at the court, where, with his bath ceremonials, Rasputin expounded his highly successful doctrine of "salvation by sin."

Favoured at first by Rasputin, who exiled him at last, he had mingled with the crafty crippled wanderers and the idiot saints in their rags and filth who had crowded the apartments of the Czar. Their mere word destroyed the ministers' plans and reports. Iliodor's story, which took one behind some of Dostoievsky's scenes, suggested a pre-Renaissance Europe surviving in our day, and, along with his disarming smile, his mind struck me as a kind of marsh into which one might sink waist-deep without reaching a bottom. I connected him with Leontyev's saying, "A Russian can be a saint but not an honest man," for one felt that some of his documents must have been forged.

Iliodor had fled to New York, where he became a Baptist and, as I heard, a janitor on the far East Side, disappearing in the vast American human ocean. But could any story have shown more clearly the inevitability of the revolution which occurred in that very year 1917, the year of the short-lived *The Seven Arts* when Russia and America seemed to be equally conscious of a new day? For the war that John Reed saw as the end of the world's youth had not destroyed in these countries hope and faith, and both saw before them what Whitman called "the wide untried domain" which the future, "greater than the past," was preparing for them. They had outgrown their provincialism, and the somewhat vague afflatus of our new magazine expressed an actual spirit in the American air, that sense of a world beginning again which had spread through Europe before the war and which the war had not killed in America or Russia. We were still living with Whitman and Morris, Ibsen, Wells, Romain Rolland, Shaw, all of whom pointed towards the future, feeling in regard to socialism that, as Anatole France remarked, it was "better to be drawn than driven to it." Every writer I came to know called himself a radical, committed to some programme for changing and improving the world. Heywood Broun spoke for them all when he said, "I hit the sawdust trail at each and every lecture" in a class in economics before which his Harvard professor asked radicals to speak; and, moreover, they had, or wished to have, the feeling of a common cause, the sense of a community of writers building a new culture.

This had been more or less Stieglitz's dream in gathering his disciples at "291," which to so many who felt at the time like pioneers in the Indian country seemed a kind of sheltering frontier fort. For the loneliness that Sherwood Anderson had found so disheartening was written all over the faces of the earlier writers, those who, like Edwin Arlington Robinson and even Theodore Dreiser, had been scouts or *avant-couriers* of the new day. I remember, at a public dinner once, sitting beside Robinson, who crouched as it were at the table with his eyes on his plate, looking up once to ask me a question to which I could only reply, "Unfortunately, no." Not another word could he be induced to utter, and he seemed as unfriended and one might say unfriendable as a frost-bitten Arctic explorer astray on an ice-floe. Then there was Theodore Dreiser, whom I first met in Patchen Place and who suggested to me some large creature of the prime wandering on the marshy plains of a human foreworld. A prognathous man with an eye askew and a paleolithic face, he put me in mind of Polyphemus,—*informe, ingens, cui lumen ademptum,*—a Rodinesque figure only half cut from the block; and yet a remark that someone made caused him to blush even up to the roots of his thin grey hair. Dreiser was hyper-sensitive, strangely as one might have thought,—he was a living paradox in more than one way; but a lonelier man there never was or one who seemed more to illustrate the need of the "growing solidarity of American writers." I am quoting a phrase of the time which expressed what its author called "a sense of their common concern, means and object."

It was largely this idea, one of the dreams of *The Seven Arts,* that brought the editors together, and Randolph Bourne, who presently joined us, hoped to form connecting links that would unite the little world of writers. Bourne had himself such a novelist's flair for personal relationships that if anyone could have done this he might have done so, realizing Henry Adams's wish for a "school" of the young that would start new influences in the country. Chekhov, who had had a similar thought, as I discovered later, had planned his "climatic station" to actualize it, appalled as he was by the bitter feuds of the coteries in St. Petersburg and feeling that writers should establish some sort of alliance. They should learn to respect one another's divergent opinions, these men "with hammers in their hands knocking at the conscience of mankind," which might have passed for Bourne's own definition. But whether in Russia or New York, this kind of "enchanted community" was of course a visionary notion, and Chekhov himself had turned against it, while our own Mencken was possibly right in saying that mutual animosity was good for writers. It was at least a sign that they took writing seriously, as Poe had taken it when he laid about him. But when so many writers were lonely and felt like aliens in their own land, the idea of a literary community was natural enough, and it comes back to me now as one of the notes of a time when many ingenuous plans were spreading about. Our decade had much in common with the New England "Newness."

I think it was to Randolph Bourne that I owed my first knowledge of Freud and Jung, to whom *The Ordeal of Mark Twain* was indebted, and *The Seven Arts* owed its existence

to these two thinkers. For the editor and the donor had been
patients of an analyst who had advised them to start it as a
therapeutic measure at a time when, as James Oppenheim
said, a day of birth seemed to be drawing near, for man was
beginning to "awaken to his planetary life." It stood for the
brotherhood of the young, Oppenheim continued, the conquest
of the world by young people of all nations when the new
writers appearing in this country might have been regarded
as the first harvest of the prophecies of Whitman. New books
were "jumping out of the press like a new dollar from a mint-
hopper," to quote David Crockett's homely phrase, books that
were no longer derivative, no longer mimetic. Romain Rolland, whose *Jean-Christophe* spoke for a super-national world
uniting the cultures of Germany, Italy and France, sent us a
message for the first issue of *The Seven Arts* bidding us, in
the name of our "Homer," to rise and act. (For Whitman, who
made one feel at home in every corner of the United States,
was the tutelary genius of the paper.) The Asiatic cultures,
China and Japan, were being born anew, Romain Rolland
said in this pronunciamento, and it was "the work of Americans" who lived at the centre of the life of the world, to
"achieve the fertile union of its great thoughts."

It must have been through Waldo Frank that this message
came to us, for Waldo was a friend already of the French
writer whom he described, in an essay on Romain Rolland, as
"the symbol of our hope . . . A world spirit speaks through
you," Waldo said, addressing him, adding that there was no
break in Rolland between recognition of a fact and whatever
words and deeds were in his power to fulfil it. This was the
case with Waldo too, as we were to see in time when he all but
invited the assaults of Argentine Fascists, and when he was
later attacked by strike-breakers in Kentucky, for he was the

most courageous of men, devoted as he was now, with all his
heart and gifts, to *The Seven Arts*. In France a long essay had
been written about him, and his book *Our America* had been
translated by Jacques Rivière, the director of the *Nouvelle
Revue Française*, while he had adopted for some of his work
the "unanimism" of Jules Romains,—in fact, he had first begun
to write in France. The world there was fashioned for the
artist and ruled by his desire, he said, and writing there was
regarded as sacramental; but, meeting French writers with a
sense that he was a parasite in their world, he had come back
to America where he felt he belonged. He had for this country a concern that was almost religious. The American artists
whom he met abroad had seldom spoken of it, and had then
spoken only to jeer and sneer, but, agreeing with much of
what they said, he had felt in their company most of all his
own compelling need of going back. Was it not the task of
artists and writers to endow the country with what they accused America of lacking?—America, that "fumbling giant
child, idealistically hungry but," as he said, "helpless to express its hunger." Anatole France, in his red skull-cap, after
inviting Waldo to call, said to him, as they sat by the open
fire, "Make no mistake. Europe is a tale that has been told.
Our long twilight is before us. But I believe in your American
dream."

Waldo, who had returned to America at the beginning of
the first world war, just when I returned,—like Randolph
Bourne,—felt, as he put it, and as many of us felt, "The
European is born on a plateau. America is still at sea-level."
For he too had grown up half a European until he discovered
Whitman and *Huckleberry Finn* at a time when there were no
little theatres, no vivid liberal weeklies, no magazines and few
books of the new type. But the more Waldo saw of the coun-

try, the more, under its "Duco finish," he felt the "dynamic impulse and the rightness of youth," as he was to observe later in *Chart for Rough Water,* and he began to share Whitman's feeling of the religious destiny that gainsaid whatever was blind and chaotic in it. Living with farmers for a while in the West, working with coal-miners, helping to edit a country newspaper in Kansas, he saw, behind the frenzied surface of the country, the secret spiritual world which the poets knew. This was the world of Jefferson, Thoreau and Ryder, and of Alfred Stieglitz, Sandburg, Robert Frost of which he wrote in *Our America.* At the same time he developed his own planetary feeling as a traveller in Palestine and Egypt, Germany and Poland. *Dawn in Russia,* one of his most spontaneous books, was a lively account of a world that was coming into being, a country of the young that was wholly moved by simple instinctive and intuitive needs in which a great spirit had been born. Waldo was deeply touched by this effort of a backward folk setting out to abolish poverty, ignorance and fear so that men might breathe the fresh air of their emotional natures. He never became a communist, and he well knew that time might twist, that inadequate ideas might destroy this dream of the moment. He was to be disillusioned by the Moscow trials. But he felt strongly the essential health of this new Russia that was so largely the result of an up-surge of youth. John Reed was a symbol there of the real America behind and beneath the "dismal claque of Business," but to Waldo the romantic Reed seemed somewhat unreal; and I remember that he seemed quite unreal to me as I watched him at *The Seven Arts* correcting proofs.

Now, on our new magazine, Waldo "yearned to join the ranks of an army" that, as he said, was "not yet in existence"; and he was looking for a criticism that would draw the battle-

line and release the young "into the joy of consecrated war."
This was the "war of a new consciousness against the forms
and language of a dying culture," and Waldo regretted that
we had no "groups" such as he had known in France, in the
circle of the Vieux Colombier theatre, for example. What a
school that had been, as we ourselves saw when it came to
New York, for the renovating of French dramatic art! Waldo
was looking for something that was alien to our Anglo-Saxon
ways, but his wish, like Randolph Bourne's, sprang from the
feeling of isolation that Waldo expressed in his novel *The
Unwelcome Man*. This was the story of Quincy Burt, who does
not fit into the American scheme, which has no place for
dreamers, for the "superfluous" people in whom lay the promise
of a richer society in the future. Feeling myself as Waldo
felt,—so largely,—about the United States, I saw in this American *Oblomov* one of those novels that were doing what the
Russian novelists had done for Russia, creating a sense of the
vacuity of their life that was sufficiently active to stimulate in
readers the desire to fill it.

Waldo as a novelist was conscientious to the last degree;
and, with his elaborate scenarios, he wrote long biographies in
advance of all the important characters in the book he was
planning. But, greatly liking some of his novels,—and the
humanity in them all,—I was always more at home with his
non-fictional writing. At first, after *The Unwelcome Man*, he
followed the method of unanimism in which the characters
were not individuals but groups,—the regiment, not the soldiers,
the soul of a room instead of the particular persons who occupied it; and, while it was obvious that *City Block* was a brilliant experiment in literary form, the people did not come alive
for me. I could not feel the impact of life in a book of which
the subject was rather the block itself than the persons in it;

and in some of the other ambitious novels I lost the sense of reality in the metaphysical atmosphere that, for me, befogged it. It seemed to me that, with all of Waldo's literary culture and distinguished mind, he was rather an intellectual than a novelist proper, though I had no such feeling in some of the less pretentious books in which he revealed himself as a simple story-teller. How good was *Summer Never Ends,* how good was *The Invaders,* a tale of atomic destruction in the second world war, and good was *Holiday* in its way too, the remarkable story of Negroes in the South that followed in the train of Gertrude Stein's *Three Lives.* Best of all, to me, was the series of tales that Waldo published years later in his book *Not Heaven,* some of which seemed to me altogether masterly and among the finest stories of our time. I mean the stories *Culture of the West, The Cat, The Last Word* and *The Kingdom of Heaven,* a terrible and wonderful tale of the Argentine pampa: stories combining in several cases fantasy and realism with a marked intensity, variety and vibrancy of style.

Waldo used to take others to task for having no philosophy. He attacked Mencken, for instance, for attacking metaphysics; and I was inclined to call this "metafussics," with the greatest of modern art critics, when he rebuked my own indifference to it. (I assume that Berenson was only referring to metaphysics in cases where he thought it out of place.) Waldo was convinced that I had no philosophy because I preferred not to appear to have one, after the fashion of the statesman who said, "My policy is to have no policy," or one might say perhaps in the manner of Sainte-Beuve (who never expressed a theory of criticism). Lincoln knew that "he did what he did because he was what he was," as one of his biographers observed, and I had a philosophy that sprang out of my whole being, but I liked to remember Goethe's remark that he "kept aloof from philosophy," preferring the "standpoint of the natural human understanding." Goethe, who said he was at home with the "common sense point of view," added that philosophical speculation had been most injurious to the Germans, tending to make their style difficult, vague and obscure; and, with the concreteness of my own mind, I could not in any case agree with Waldo's philosophy or metaphysics. It sprang from the Jewish prophetic tradition in its mediæval form, and this allied Waldo to the neo-scholastics, with whom he deplored the descent of man since the old "Catholic synthesis," regarding the modern age as a decline and fall. To Waldo the Enlightenment was shallow because it omitted the divine from its notion of man, whereas nothing could persuade me that in the long run humanism would fail to include every human value. I was convinced that humankind was moving towards a synthesis that would make mediæval Europe seem parochial in contrast.

Literature to Waldo was religious or nothing, and most of the good writers of the time were therefore, from his point of view, creators of "gilded" fiction or decorators merely. He felt they had scarcely more sense that life has a purpose and direction than the "impotent intellectuals of the Café du Dôme." They went along with a civilization that was "top-heavy with machines" and run by machine-minded and machine-exhausted men, and he was drawn to Latin America because, whatever were its defects, "well-being" was not considered the highest good there. It seemed to him obvious that certain values survived in the Hispanic scene that our country had forgotten almost since the days of Roger Williams, for the mystical tradition, the "great tradition" had largely vanished from our general mind, where it had been replaced by the practical tradition. Waldo never lost faith in this country, which he described as "capturable," saying, "There is a bloom within our land which Europe lacks, a generosity and the faith and will which flower from it"; but, feeling that the mystical values flourished still in the Hispanic world, he hoped for a cultural union between the North and the South. Believing that this would restore the traditional wholeness of man, he set out to interpret these worlds to one another, an undertaking of twenty years that produced what seemed to me Waldo's most significant series of books.

He first encountered in the closing year of *The Seven Arts* a poor and exiled fragment of the world of the Spaniards when, in our own Southwest, he had sensed at once that it had something for him and for our people. It was something the absence of which made our proud industrial world, with all its triumphant successes, a danger and delusion, as Waldo wrote later in *South American Journey,* and his intuition soon sent him to Spain, and later to Mexico and Argentina, to find the source of strength this world possessed. It was then he wrote *Virgin Spain,* so full of poetic perception, with its real understanding of the mystical tradition that our practical business world had so wholly lost sight of,—the first, after *Our America*, of the "New World" series that even included his *Bolivar* of years to come. For, seeing in Spain the source of the civilization of Latin America, he saw in this what Bolivar envisaged, one half of the Atlantic world, an organic body, whole and free, an America stretching from the Arctic down to the Horn. This was the world of which Juarez and Lincoln were equally creators, foretold by the New England prophets as by Sarmiento, a world more propitious for the family of man than the old world had ever been, embodying a new sensibility and a new culture.

As a literary ambassador to Latin America Waldo was unique, for there could scarcely ever have been another North

American who was able to enter that world by his deep inner
line. No one could have differed more from the usual type
of American who represented the threat of the big business
of the North; and, knowing Spain first, he was at home with
Spaniard, mestizo and Indian alike, loving their dances, their
religion, the form of their minds. Along with them he hated
their own corrupt governments, in league with sinister elements
in this country, and with his ardour of spirit and concern for
justice, he entered sympathetically all their minds. He knew
the great cultural regions of the Caribbean, the Amazon, the
Andes and the pampa, which he presented in his most moving
prose, together with the secret Indian life that lay behind them
all with its memories of great cultures of the past. He brought
before his readers the Venezuelan forest, the mountains and
the jungle of the Orinoco, and he who had known so well the
writers and writing of modern Spain knew better the writers
of Peru, Argentina, Chile. He brought his own countrymen
their first news of the vivid intellectual life of the South, while
he was the Balzac, I have been told by one who was in a position to know, of a whole school of novelists in Argentina. On
his triumphal tours he went far to convince each world that it
needed the other to complete it,—the cultures of "bread-and-
power" and "art-and-religion,"—while he brought the South
Americans the picture of a life in the United States that was
remote indeed from the world of the dollar. This was the life
of the Puritan mystics, as of Emerson, Thoreau, Whitman
and their successors in our time.

I would be looking too far ahead if, in the days of *The Seven
Arts,* all this had not been latent in Waldo's writing and if he
had not discovered for the magazine so many "seeds beneath
the snow." Meanwhile, John Dewey wrote for us, "The war has
shown that we are a new body and a new spirit in the world,"

and it was the hope of developing this that brought us all together, Waldo, Randolph Bourne and the rest of the circle. Especially Louis Untermeyer, Amy Lowell's rival as the spokesman of the "poetry Renaissance," whose great point was that American poetry had ceased to be an escape from life and had become a "spirited encounter with it." To the advancement of this cause Louis brought, first, a catholic taste and, secondly, a peculiar sagacity and wit. As for Randolph Bourne, I had known him for two or three years before we were connected with *The Seven Arts*. He had been writing articles of a personal philosophy, with others about what he called the "school of tomorrow," and we talked and corresponded on the question of bringing writers together, all the more vital in the engulfing blackness of the war. Randolph was obsessed with a sense that we were all "aliens."

Here, as I remember it, he expressed a feeling that most of the writers and artists shared at the moment: what did they have in common with the world as they knew it? Few felt at home in what Tawney called the "acquisitive society," the world of Matthew Josephson's "Robber Barons," and, ever since Edwin Arlington Robinson had said in his boyhood "Business be damned," writers had been repeating this over and over. Had not Henry Adams pointed out how the "bankers" had betrayed the republic? Had not Brooks Adams observed that the "principle of evil" was embodied in the "greed and avarice" of competition? Ezra Pound was on the point of saying that the "usurers" betrayed everything that writers and artists cared for,—those heroes of the big-business world whom the muck-rakers had abused and exposed and whom Waldo Frank attacked with O'Neill and Dos Passos? All these writers were in revolt against what Waldo called the "cold lethal simplicities of American business culture," the monstrous disproportion between business and the other concerns of life in E. E. Cummings's "land of the Cluett shirt." What, in Edmund Wilson's jingle, had this made of the American man?—

> With his seven motor-cars,
> His twenty kinds of peanut bars,
> His fifty different sorts of hose
> And eighty makes of underclothes.

No imaginative mind could think very much of that. Meanwhile, Veblen had convinced the young that business itself was perverse, and that its ways were inexpedient also, in contrast to the ways of industry, properly managed; and Sherwood Anderson's famous flight, when he "walked out" of his office, had become the symbol of an epoch. Waldo Frank used this theme in *The Death and Birth of David Markand* as well as in *Summer Never Ends,* the heroes of which in both cases abandoned their careers to find their souls in a world remote from "success." If most of the writers were socialists, was this not, precisely, what Henry Adams said he "should have been"? In spite of what Walt Whitman called the "caterwauling" of the radicals and their "unceasing complaints against everything," Whitman had remained a radical with socialist leanings; and so had Randolph Bourne, and so had I.

Bourne himself was the perfect type of the "clerc" of Julien Benda, the dedicated "enlightened man," the true-blue intellectual, a word that had only recently come into use. It had with us a colour of the Russian intelligentsia, the word for those who, in Russia, formed public opinion and one that practically meant there the heirs of the Enlightenment who believed in perfectibility and human evolution. They were opposed, by definition, to the ideas of orthodoxy, authority, censorship, reaction, repression and so on,—everything that Iliodor represented,—believers in progress that they were, in

the natural goodness of men and the heritage of the age of
revolution. In France, Julien Benda used the word "clerc" in
the same sense, and the *trahison des clercs* of which he was
presently to write was largely treason against this mental outlook.
It was the "effort to discourage hope" of the new "romantics of pessimism" with their doctrine of the incurable wickedness of man, those who enjoyed their own "contempt for
others," a feeling that always appealed to the "elegant herd."
Their treason consisted in the pleasure they found in laughing
at the naive souls who thought that some day humanity might
"become better." When at last Benda's book came out, virtually
all the serious writers accepted this definition of the *clerc,*
which embodied their own conception of literary ethics, as anyone, looking back, could see in old numbers of *The New Republic, The Seven Arts, The Nation* or *The Dial*. Bourne
could never have dreamed of the change in the literary climate
of the country that was to take place in decades to come when,
following T. E. Hulme and T. S. Eliot especially, the bright
young people reversed this point of view. What Benda had
called treason they regarded as the true faith: the denial of
progress, pessimism, the incurable wickedness of man and all
the other notions of the neo-scholastics. They followed the
"dignified landlady," Eliot,—in Miss Kathleen Nott's phrase,—
who "retrieved the tribal ornaments from the cupboard where
the guest had hidden them" and quietly "put them back on
the mantelpiece."

These clercs-in-reverse of the future might have had a more
difficult victory if Bourne had lived long enough to counter-
attack them, feeling perhaps that what Benda described as a
certain "barbarity of heart" lay at the root of what he called
their treason. He might even have made short work of those
who found it so pleasing to picture mankind as walled in by an

eternal and inevitable woe; for he was a formidable adversary of the type of the Encyclopædists, tough-minded and both humane and ironical also. He was even rather like Voltaire in his vivid appeal to the other sex. Numbers of women shrank from Bourne, but others, beautiful and young, were fascinated by the "tiny, twisted, unscared" creature in "his black cloak hopping alone," as John Dos Passos remembered him in *U.S.A.*, the "frightening dwarf" from whom Theodore Dreiser recoiled, one shadowy winter night, on a corner in Greenwich Village in the snow. A chill passed over Dreiser at his first glimpse of Bourne's long arms, his crooked head sunk deep between bony shoulders, with the large ears flattened against the skull, but, meeting this cripple by daylight and talking with him, he could see only Bourne's large clear intelligent eyes. After that he never saw the dwarf in Bourne at all: he saw a powerful body that matched the mind whose literary power with its clarity of thinking impressed Willa Cather too, as it came up fresh and green like marsh-grass under water.

Bourne was even a romantic figure, especially when he was playing Brahms with the "nineteenth-century affection for the piano" that his great friend Paul Rosenfeld ascribed to himself; and for a walking tour he was the perfect companion, as I found when we walked out to Provincetown together. His steps were as quick as a robin's, his spirits never flagged, and he explored every by-way, eagerly scenting the honeysuckle, the bay-leaves and the salt air of the Cape. With him, at Provincetown, I spent an hour with Eugene O'Neill, my first and only meeting with this wonder of the stage who had written for *The Seven Arts* a story that might have been the first sketch of a number of his plays. Before we set out for the Cape we had spent a day in Boston, and, strolling through the old squares and streets roundabout Beacon Hill, I realized for the first time the charm of the town. It seems to me, as I look back, that I had passed through Harvard without in the least perceiving its unity and grace, unique in American cities and to me enchanting; and I feel that I owe to Randolph Bourne my first real discovery of a town that was to mean much to me twenty years later. To style in any form he was acutely responsive.

That was in August, 1917, four months after this country had entered the war, and Bourne, as a dogged pacifist who actively opposed the war, was under the surveillance of the police. It was his writing largely that killed *The Seven Arts*, for the donor could not accept this anti-war position, nor could I, for it seemed to me that to oppose the war was scarcely less futile than opposing an earthquake. Besides, was not Pan-Germanism a terrible menace? I felt rather as John Sloan felt when he left *The Masses* at about this time because that paper also went in for propaganda, attacking the war in a dogmatic fashion; and, like him, I could not see why a magazine that served the arts should throw away its life for any such reason. But Randolph was impelled to oppose the war,—he shrank from violence and force all the more because of his physical weakness; and he recalled at this time Thoreau who had similarly opposed the Mexican war, remarking that his thoughts were "murder to the state."

Bourne said the war outlawed anyone who followed a non-conformist line and refused to act as a symbol of society's folk-ways, and, with his own animus against what he called the war-mind, he had taken more and more to political writing. War, for him, was the "health of the state" and dissent was like sand in the bearings of the great herd-machine that was on the rampage, and he grieved because the universities were driving into limbo those who tried to exercise their minds.

Veblen's was the only intelligent effort in the country that was not running to war-propaganda, while in England, in spite of all repression, speculative thought continued to thrive and even, during the war, with increasing boldness. For Bourne the war meant the end of American promise; it was driving everything he valued into the sea; and he was regarded as a sinister person, dangerous perhaps, who was shadowed by government detectives. During a submarine scare, on a headland that overlooked Buzzard's Bay, they suddenly rose out of the ground and questioned him, and he was asked on another occasion to explain the French word *perfide* which one of his friends used in a telegram. Did not some dark secret lurk behind it? A real blow followed when a trunk that was filled with his manuscripts vanished between New York and the beach near by where he spent the last summer of his life with my wife and me. This trunk was never recovered, and the general understanding was that it could not have disappeared unless it had been confiscated by governmental agents.

About this time Hendrik van Loon was also shadowed by the police, as I became aware when I was with him, because what he rightly called his plain old-fashioned liberalism had been taken for the pro-Germanism that was treason at the moment. This, he was convinced, was because he clicked his heels together when he was bowing over a lady's hand, for he had spent five years in Germany and Austria and taken a doctor's degree at the University of Munich. Then he was suspected of "Bolshevism" because a Russian dictionary was found in his rooms, the result of an early ambition to become a famous linguist that had also led him into Arabic and Japanese. This was supposed to be highly irregular and his lodgings were broken into, his trunks were opened by detectives and his mail was stolen. Hendrik too I had first met in the office of

*The Seven Arts,* where he sat on a big table swinging his legs, describing his night in a lifeboat in the English Channel when his ship had been torpedoed. He had been the only correspondent in Antwerp during the siege. Hendrik had not yet written the books that were to make him widely known, but I vividly remember this first glimpse of a man I was to know well when he came to live in Westport later.

## CHAPTER III

# A FAMILY STORY

To speak for a moment of personal affairs, my wife, whose name was Eleanor Stimson, was the only daughter of two artists. Her father was John Ward Stimson, who had founded in the eighteen-eighties the art school of the Metropolitan Museum in New York, and he had met her mother at the Art Students' League where for a while he taught and she was a pupil. At that time story pictures were the vogue, with period costumes and "ideal" nudes, anecdotes and Barbizon pastoral scenes, and the two shared for a dozen years a more or less idyllic life before they decided to follow separate ways. My wife was accustomed early to a wandering existence. Her father had spent seven years in Paris and her mother had studied in Europe too, living for a year, as a girl, in Turin with Louis Kossuth's sister, Madame Ruttkay, the ancient friend of Miss Kenyon, her aunt. From the patriarch himself she had learned the games of solitaire that she so constantly played as she roamed about the world, games that, as a younger man, Kossuth had invented in order to while away his time in prison. My mother-in-law whiled away her time in painting,—fields of wild flowers, mountain slopes and what not,—wherever she happened to be, seated in a camp-chair, under an umbrella, swathed in veils, with a big straw hat, as if she were posing for a Sargent water-colour.

I had entered this picture early in life, for my mother-in-law and my mother had been school friends at the Seminary of my *Scenes and Portraits,* and we had all gone abroad together when my wife was a little girl and when I was to see my burning bush in Dresden. The little girl had lived, for several years, at Saranac before the débâcle of her family when her father was ill,—in Robert Louis Stevenson's cottage for a part of a year,—and there she had acquired a love of the woods, of tents and camping out, that she was to share later with her children. We were always to have tents stowed away, one glorified tent in particular that might have suited Saladin on campaign,—a canvas house with extensions for platforms and tables,—ready for a fortnight on Big Moose Lake or in the high Sierras or, if such things were possible, in the Swiss mountains. For Lausanne, where my wife went to school, was only a prelusive taste of other later Alpine years or summers, in châlets and hotels at Wengen or Mürren, on the Lac de Champex once or twice or in the valley of the Rhone. She had loved to build fires in the open and clamber over snow-fields in days when there was time for everything and one could spend hours in sunny clearings reading or watching the insects or listening, by some wild stream, to the summer sounds. Or feeling the earth move under her, with a furious secret rush through space, for she shared Whitman's "cosmic" intuition. She could have drawn from memory later almost every peak in certain parts, at least, of Switzerland, and she could have told you just how low the shadows fell in the afternoon and when the Alpenglow was at its height.

After our marriage at Carmel, we were to spend our honeymoon tenting in the Yosemite valley, on the bank of the river,—where I learned how to boil an egg and she to poach one,—and this was a reminiscence of the Adirondack years

when my wife had not yet gone with her mother to Europe.
Before and after she came home to go through Wellesley College, she had lived in hotels and pensions in three or four
countries,—with paint-boxes, spirit-lamps and travelling clocks,
—learning Italian in Capri and spending three years in Paris,
where her brother was studying architecture. I was in England
then and we were often together on both sides of the channel.
I remember days in Epping Forest under the great beech trees
and others at Versailles in the autumn woods, old dull gold in
colour, wonderful at twilight. There one found little marble
pools with marble fauns beside them, half covered with the
red leaves that carpeted the ground. We were both in love with
Europe and always had been. But it comes back to me now that
my wife's deep pride of country had thriven all the more in
her wandering existence. This pride, which had no element of
chauvinism in it, produced in the end a profound effect on
me, and so did her mystical faith in mankind and its future.

Every August, for many years, we spent a few days at East
Hampton, where the Stimsons had immemorially passed their
summers, living with patriarchal simplicity and old-fashioned
elegance in their ample unpretentious Gothic villa. Henry L.
Stimson, the statesman, a cousin of my wife and the head of
the clan after the last uncle's death at ninety-six, often appeared from High Hold, far up Long Island, also drawn there
by the surviving aunts. It was from them we heard the family
stories that aunts, and aunts alone, seem to remember, tales
of the Boudinot brothers and the Peartree Smiths, one of
whom had been painted by Sir Godfrey Kneller. This forbear
had been governor of Jamaica in the days of Queen Anne.
Then there were stories of the Audubon cousins, for another
aunt, more than a century back, had married the romantic
French woodsman, the Columbus of the birds, and my mother-

in-law remembered calling on his children at Minnie's Land, their old place on the Hudson. We heard much more of the Boudinots, one of whom had been offered a dukedom, during the Revolution, by agents of the British, if he could persuade the rebels to make peace with the king, for he had been president of the Continental Congress. Nothing, he wrote to his wife, could have interested him less. But the tragedy of the Stimsons, one of them remarked, was that they were descended from the wrong Boudinot brother. It was Elias who was offered the dukedom, and it was at Elias's house that the father of his country spent the night before his inauguration. However, Elisha made a good showing in Congress, and his daughter, aged five, was the one whom George Washington tossed in his arms as he called her "My little yellow bird." For the child wore at the moment a yellow frock. Later, Alexander Hamilton was the best man at her wedding when this grandmother of my children's great-grandmother finally grew up,—one of a score of similar tales that seemed to carry us very far from the foreground of our Westport life among the artists.

But East Hampton, too, had been an artists' colony like the Norman fishing villages of Étretat and Deauville before they were taken over by the world of fashion, and there still lived Thomas Moran, my father-in-law's ancient friend, the painter of Turneresque sunsets and Western mountains. In the garden of this brisk old man,—short and slight, with a prophet's beard,—lay Robert Browning's gondola, brought over from Venice long after Saint-Gaudens and Alden Weir, E. A. Abbey and William M. Chase had all foregathered near the village duck-pond. They had found touches of Europe there, for they could see America only when they saw it as European, and the lanes brought back England to some of them, while the dunes and windmills suggested Holland and the meadows recalled to others Pont-Aven. At the time my father and mother-in-law had carried on summer sketch classes, mainly for young ladies who had also come down from New York, and they had their studio in the old Clinton Academy where the father of John Howard Payne had once been a teacher. On the bare oaken floor stood the Windsor chairs, the spinning-wheels and the schoolmaster's desk they had found in the loft, and they hung on the walls, among sketches and studies, the costumes, poke-bonnets and fishing-tackle, the reels, nets and anchors they liked to paint. These were the seaside equivalents of the tambourines and round brass plaques, the satin banners painted with chrysanthemums and roses, the decorated earthen pots and the bits of old copper and silver that were dear to so many artists at the moment in the city. Long years were to pass before any of these innocents found themselves obliged to reckon with Matisse and Picasso.

Meanwhile, my own old friend the poet John Hall Wheelock had roamed from his earliest childhood the great island beaches, the scene of so many of his poems, early and late, where I often went for a swim with him and once with his uncle Bolton Hall, who had known all the old East Hampton artists. This great Tolstoyan was eighty at the time, but, unwilling to yield to the unwelcome fact, he disported himself in the surf while Jack hovered in the waves around and beside him. He was keeping a protective eye on the adventurous elder. Said Bolton Hall to me, as he cavorted on the top of a wave, "I can teach anyone to swim in a single lesson" . . . "Why, Mr. Hall," said I, "how can you do that?" . . . "By giving him confidence," the ancient replied, taking a header into a wave, from which he emerged defiantly half a minute later. Still the vigilant nephew swam beside him, like an anxious parent duck with one of the chicks.

But, to return to my father-in-law, whatever had become of him, that figure of mystery whom I had never met?

One day, in Westport, as I passed the house of Guy Pène du Bois, I noticed on the adjoining lawn twenty or thirty canvasses that were spread out as if to catch the sun. The owner, a minor official of one of the academies in New York who had known Blakelock before he was sent to the asylum, remembering that he had stowed in his attic all these pictures by his old friend, had brought them down to look them over. And perhaps even to sell them, in the flurry of Blakelock's sudden fame, if the sunlight would brighten them a little; for the painter had used so much bitumen to give them an amber look of age that many of them had turned black altogether. One caught in them here and there the yellow brown and russet notes that characterized George Fuller and Ryder also, with whom the rare good Blakelocks had much in common, but one realized *how* rare these had been and how often the artist had gone astray in the aesthetic twilight of his generation. The pictures, moreover, reminded me of the work of my father-in-law, which I had known well though I had not known him,—pictures that might have been Blakelock's or his old friend D. L. Tryon's, for they were all of the same school and the same epoch. They were all productions of a day when the Goncourts wrote in their journal, *"Le paysage est la victoire de l'art moderne"*; but my father-in-law's pictures too had been banished, they had lived an unsunned attic life, except for the few one saw in obscure museums. He himself seemed to me a symbol of the American artist's fate in the shadowy unrequiting generation when so many who had studied in Paris under the spell of the Barbizon school had struggled to survive in their age of innocence at home.

I sometimes had letters from my father-in-law, for he still

lived in the far West, having broken with his early connections and drifted away there. A graduate of Yale, he had been a rebel in his patrician family's house, and, returning from a long stay in France, he had painted round about New York before he set up as a teacher and aesthetic prophet. Leaving the Metropolitan school, he had established a school of his own, the Artist-Artisan Institute in West Twenty-third Street, where for five years Henry McBride, the champion later of "modern" art, who followed him to Trenton, had been his assistant. Then he had gone West to the "psychic belt" of southern California, the final abode of many another prophet. At times he believed that his great work was universally recognized and he basked in a half-fanciful sense of his own glory, while at other times, like Gauguin, whom he resembled in photographs, he saw himself as a martyr, crucified. With his beak of a nose, wild eyes and flowing moustaches, he combined the brown velveteen jacket of the romantic artist, and the Eastern painters he had left behind were automatons from his point of view, poseurs, little prigs, geese or blockheads. Reading his letters and papers later, I found myself sharing in scenes of which I had caught only glimpses elsewhere.

He had gone to Paris in 1872 when Meissonier was one of the reigning talents, with Bouguereau and Cabanel, the painter of "conscientious" nudes, who was to become presently his own teacher. Living, as he wrote, "with Turgot-like prudence and Walpole-like economy," at least regarding his lodgings in the Hotel de Sparte, he kept in touch with the world at home by reading *The Nation* every week, the journal of the intelligentsia in Boston and New York. With a friend from Yale and a Glasgow boy, a Scottish fellow-student with whom he exchanged national poets, Longfellow for Burns, he formed one of a trio like Trilby's admirers and wore side-whiskers some of the time before he acquired the imperial he brought back from France. The ruins of the Franco-Prussian war were still to be found on all sides, with the great black crater of the Tuileries which he passed every day and the bullet-riddled front of his hotel, while in the Luxembourg gardens one saw the marks of the bullets on the wall against which the Communist leaders had been shot. There was a cyclorama in the Champs-Elysées within which, standing on what seemed to be a bastion of Fort Issy, one found oneself in the midst of the siege of Paris. It was not easy for him to explain why, after the Germans had won the war, President Grant had congratulated Bismarck, considering the old friendship of France and the United States, and my father-in-law was constantly struck by the patient good humour of the French, their courtesy, self-reliance, pertinacity and thrift. For the rest, he delighted in the tumbledown alleys in Paris and the picturesque types he saw on the streets, the beetle-winged bonnets from Alsace, the broad brims from Brittany, the soldiers in jack-boots, the priests in slippers. On Sundays, he wrote to his grandmother, he took John Woolman's Journal and walked out to the Bois de Boulogne to read it. I wondered, reading his letters, if he had met my father, who spent five years in Paris at the same time, a time when Henry James had found it the best of meeting-places in which to observe his countrymen abroad.

Under and behind everything there, my father-in-law felt the smouldering terror that was buried in the communistic hordes. "We live on the slopes of Vesuvius," he wrote, "in Paris." When he was out of town his friends narrated in letters to him the jokes and scandals in the studios and the rivalries between them, the news of the atelier of Jean Paul Laurens together with the protracted rows between the Atelier Cabanel and the Atelier Gérôme. Both the latter were obliged to close.

The Gérômites broke down the door to get their painting-boxes, and the sculptor Saint-Gaudens, reappearing in Paris, went in to see his brother and had his own coat torn in the mêlée that followed. My father-in-law, toiling away under the meticulous Cabanel,—that "mud-god of art," as Huneker called him,—soon won a medal at the Beaux-Arts for his academic drawing. Being "well-grounded in 'light and shadow,'" learning to "express solid form before giving much time to colour,"—it was obvious to him,—was "the key of all future successful work . . . Colour comes naturally and easily after the groundwork has been safely laid, while the jumping forward with too much impatience into a subsequent field has been the ruin of many a promising young talent." But, gladly accepting this discipline, my father-in-law broke away from the Beaux-Arts ideality and classical manner, immensely taken as he was with a great show-piece by Rosa Bonheur of reapers bringing home the hay in the summer twilight. He could not say enough in praise of the huge lumbering wain, the farmers walking beside it with their scythes and rakes, the soft glow of the evening sky and the oxen so painted to the life that one could almost feel their fragrant breath.

My father-in-law had fallen in with a current vogue in Paris, a taste that was universal in the art-world of the moment, and the feeling for this subject, better expressed by Millet on his farm at Fontainebleau, appeared in my father-in-law's own later painting. He was drawn, like so many in the seventies, to the poetry of the common life, in hamlets, on farms, among simple people, especially after a magical summer he spent at Vézelay, the ancient feudal village in the department of Yonne. It was far from any railroad, no tourists came there, and the big kitchen of the inn swarmed with farmers at the end of the day rubbing their elbows on the table and pounding with their glasses. They were gossipy strapping Burgundian duffers with whips and massive sabots or huge boots steaming from the cow-yard, and their guffaws rang down the road as their bellies pressed against the board and they drained their tumblers of the red Bourgogne. My father-in-law and his fellow-students had the inn all to themselves, only disturbed when the widow and children of the famous Montalembert arrived in the middle of the summer for a short visit,—they were obliged to sacrifice their sofa for one of the young marquises to sleep on. What suggestive and interesting subjects the broken landscape offered them, especially the peasants in the fields or during the vintage when the leaves turned to a thousand hues and tossed in the frosty autumn wind. Then groups of the peasants bent over the vines or loaded the baskets they bore on their backs with full clusters of grapes to be trampled in the cellars. My father-in-law delighted in these open-hearted kindly men, stout as Old King Cole in the story-book, as he watched the red blood of the grapes spurting under their sinewy legs and pouring into the big oaken receivers. It was a fine sight in the gloom of the vast stone cellars under the massive arches built by monks; and these men understood an artist's interest in their work and were always ready for a visit from Monsieur Jean.

There he studied sunlight and its wonderful effects on form, rejoicing in the full panorama of a clear day from the first grey flashes of sunrise to the final evening glow, followed by the cool moon and the silhouettes of shadows. Meanwhile, he loved to pass an hour with old Mère Catherine, the mother of the village shoemaker, in her one-room cottage, with baskets and old pots hanging from the rafters while she sewed or sat at the spinning-wheel. He enjoyed her droll homely sayings and Burgundian wit, and he joined her and her son at the feast of St. Crépin, the shoemaker's patron, when they sat round a rickety candle at the well-scrubbed board. They had cabbage soup followed by the rabbit which the son had killed in the back yard, with a loaf of brown bread and some old wine stamped out by mother and son and kept in the cellar, and they drank the health of all honest people everywhere, especially if they were good republicans. For the election was coming on and in this department, a Bonapartist stronghold, the republic was fighting for its life. My father-in-law took part in the speech-making. He was more impressed than ever by the calm self-control of the French when their national life seemed to be at stake.

It was in 1879 that he returned to New York, finding himself disturbed, as he wrote, by the bumptious ignorance, sharpness and cheek and the monetary standard of merit that seemed to prevail there. For the rest, he found what Gauguin found in Copenhagen, the circumscribed, starched, self-righteous life of conventional people everywhere that Americans sometimes thought peculiar to themselves. He had spent eight months in Naples and in Venice, surrounded by Tintoretto's "dreams of a giant," painting himself in the grand style that he had also acquired in France, with biblical, architectural and animal subjects. He had crossed the battlefield of Sédan where the ruins of villages lay untouched and torn shreds of blue coats and old army boots still lay about, and, painting landscapes here and there, he had tramped in Switzerland with rhododendron blossoms stuck in his hat. He had walked across Belgium and Holland, full of impressions, enough, he wrote, to "burst like a Dutch dyke," and settling at home, for a while at East Hampton, near his family's summer house, he began to look for the scenes he had loved in Europe. "You do not affiliate with the 'poor rustics,' " he wrote to his mother from New York,

"though they have lots of interest in them, good hearts, experience, mother wit and character for him who is willing to 'see' ";
and he saw, or wished to see, Burgundian peasants and Mère Catherines in the farming and fishing folk gathering their sea-moss. He wrote, "It is our mission as artists today to see the poetry of simple things," and he looked for this in the clover-fields environing the village, oases in the sandy Long Island waste. He painted farm-yards at Montauk, green meadows with grazing cows, ducks leading their broods over the common, scythes hanging from the branches of willow-trees and picturesque old cottages, especially Payne's original "Home Sweet Home." Like Ludlow, the painter, in Howells's novel *The Coast of Bohemia,* who had also just returned from Paris, he was "eager to report the native world on canvas and draw as much pathos out of the farm-folk as Millet had ever drawn from the Barbizon peasants."

When I happened on this novel, it seemed to me that Howells must surely have had in mind my father-in-law, for the fictional artist so greatly resembled the real one who had also painted in the *plein air* of France. Under the American sky again, both were bent on "proving that our life is full of poetry and picturesqueness,"—I am quoting Ludlow's remark in Howells's novel,—and both were full of the great problem "of the relation of our art to our life," while they were equally obliged to contend with "blockheads." For both found themselves at odds with the teaching of the Art Students' League,—the Synthesis, so called, in Howells's novel,—the wooden mechanical system that my father-in-law contrasted with "plastic vitality and truth to organic form." They were both exasperated by the vague shallow talk about art that had been going on for a decade or more and they were determined to celebrate the native world that others saw in terms of Brittany, Normandy, Holland or England. Delighting in the old houses, with their brick ovens, kettles and cranes, "so full of artistic suggestions," as one of them remarked, they persisted in their search for what my father-in-law described as "sincere American beauty and inspiration."

Sketching and painting himself, meanwhile,—haycocks and weather-beaten barns, farm-kitchens, scenes of autumn threshing,—my father-in-law was greatly concerned with what he called vital art education and the writing and teaching that expressed his interest in it. Returning from Europe, he had missed the *esprit de corps* that he had found or felt among artists in Paris, while he set out to fight the apathetic patriots who hoped for nothing good in their Nazareth at home. He began to agitate for a national art society to benefit the genius of the country and its tastes and outlook, his great point being that the gap should be closed between the fine and the industrial arts, that artists and artisan should work together. Moreover, whatever a man's life was, he should love his work with artistic pride, for its own sake and not for the profit of it. He had to contend, he wrote, with cliques and self-interested snobs and self-righteous committees, but he never doubted that his was the wave of the future. "We are, I take it, just now in the trough of the sea of progress, but the young men are already born who will ride on the crest of the coming wave." Meanwhile, publishing his essays and poems in *The Studio* and other magazines, he examined American Indian pottery and painting, implements, fabrics, artifacts of the Stone and the Bronze age, which he used in the illustrations of his huge book on the principles of art, tracing to natural forms the elements of design. For, as a mystic, he was convinced that every design mankind has evolved has been based on some aspect of the universe, a snow-crystal or a leaf, or perhaps even a constellation, that there exists a harmony between the universe itself and everything men have devised in colour and line.

Far away and long ago seemed this great age of the isms that my father-in-law's letters and papers opened to me, the days when I had been a child and when Utopia seemed close at hand and benevolent motives governed every thinker. For that was the time not only of Tolstoy in Russia but of Edward Bellamy and Henry George at home. As director of the art school of the Metropolitan Museum, my father-in-law had had a resounding success,—the number of pupils rose from forty to four hundred,—while he taught drawing and composition with Olin Warner, Elihu Vedder and William Hamilton Gibson among his assistants. There were classes in decorative design, glass-making, wood-carving and work in brass as well as in painting, sculpture and architecture, and these had been continued at the Artist-Artisan Institute, my father-in-law's own special and personal school. "There is a great movement going on in the United States," Edward Carpenter wrote to him from England, "an immensely rapid uprise in educational, social and transcendental planes of thought, which will not fail, I think, to produce a wonderful people before long; and I congratulate you on your share in the great work." Walter Crane also wrote to tell him about the similar work which the Arts and Crafts movement was doing in England, and letters of friendship and gratitude came from Frederick J. Church and Saint-Gaudens, "Jenny June" Croly and many another. Charles Dudley Warner was full of praise for his "effort to make art a part of our national life," and Hamlin Garland wrote to him and Edwin Markham thanked him for "sowing seed for a future civilization." His philosophy appealed to a few minds in all corners of the world. My father-in-law had written his book when he was ill and in exile, in bleak and dreary days of driving snow, sure that it consisted of sacred revelations which he had spread abroad to help mankind. When Sun Yat Sen wrote to him from China and the poet Tagore from India, he recalled the prophecy that had moved him when he was at work, "Go forth, weeping, bearing precious seed, and thou shalt surely return rejoicing, bringing thy sheathes with thee."

Many years after the twenties and the heyday of *The Dial*, of which Henry McBride had been the art critic, I asked this great discoverer of so many talents of our own day how he regarded the old artist who had been his teacher. My father-in-law's painting, so good at first, in Blakelock's or George Fuller's way, had lost its depth and glow before he vanished, like Lao-tsze, into the West, and his career as a painter recalled to me the classic case, so often repeated in America, of Washington Allston. It exemplified all the old warnings of so many critics about the fate of the artist in our undeveloped country, and it was in my mind no doubt in all my speculations regarding the "problem," as we saw it, of the American writer. At the same time, my father-in-law had anticipated many of our own thoughts, those of my friends and myself, in the early twenties, concerning the relation of American art to American life, for example, and the question of evolving a national from a colonial outlook. But how did Henry McBride regard this wild and fiery aristocrat as a man and a teacher?—this lover of Blake who detested the fashionable Sargent and who wished to upset the academies and all they stood for. He was "a genius, —*manqué* but unmistakable," Henry McBride said, looking back. For the rest, I saw in my father-in-law a mind that was born too soon and that might have fared better in our own twenties, when, as Henry McBride remarked in another connection, "Everything was coming up. You felt it."

CHAPTER IV

# THE FREEMAN

R ANDOLPH BOURNE had been dead two years when I went to
live in Westport, and just at that moment, in 1920, appeared a new weekly, *The Freeman,* of which I was the literary
editor for most of a lustrum. This was the creation of two ill-
assorted but remarkable men, a recessive American, Albert Jay
Nock, who was stoical, dry and laconic, and a romantic Englishman, Francis Neilson. I was busy every week two or three
days in the office in New York, but I wrote my reviews and
articles at home.

It was Albert Nock, the actual editor, with whom I dealt
day by day, while Francis Neilson, who was living in Chicago,
appeared at the office only from time to time. A member of
Parliament in England once and the stage-director at Covent
Garden, he had been as a young man an actor in both London
and New York, where he knew the Broadway of Huneker's
time; and he had been as much at home in the old Bohemia
of Union Square as he was now, on visits, in his rooms at the
Ritz. For he had married a daughter of Gustavus Swift, who
financed *The Freeman* as a sort of plaything for him. A friend
of Anton Seidl, who had been Wagner's right-hand man, he
had scoured Munich and Salzburg, Berlin, Vienna and Buda-
pest in search of new talent for his own opera in London. A
prolific librettist and playwright, he had written *The Butterfly*

*on the Wheel* with various other plays, some of them in French, among them *Le Baiser de Sang* at the Grand Guignol. The actors, at lunch with him, had said they needed a good play, and he replied, "Come to lunch tomorrow and I will have one for you." His play had had the longest run of any ever produced at this theatre in Paris. But he struck a true English note when he said there was nothing so wonderful as a blackbird in full song in a garden in the country.

A florid expansive Wiltshire man, Neilson had studied Henry George, a favourite of many old actors in the eighties and nineties, and he had fallen in with Nock because this American journalist was also devoted to "fundamental economics." Choosing Nock for an editor, he had also met with the publisher of my *Letters and Leadership* and *America's Coming-of-Age,* one of those publishers by vocation of whom four or five appeared as another note of this time of awakening in letters. With so much experimentation among novelists and poets, with little theatres opening all over the country and with competitions for stories and for painting and music, it was quite natural that these publishers should have sprung up too, representing a new type and outlook. For, with small hope of profit, they brought out books for the fun of it, out of sheer love for literature and beautiful designing, or, in advance of the older publishers, they foresaw the profit that was sure to accrue from the new great audience and the many new authors. B. W. Huebsch, later of the Viking Press but now with a publishing house of his own, was a cultivated lover of music who could also, on occasion, turn out an admirable essay on a literary subject. Like Neilson, the *bon viveur,* and the severe and disciplined Nock, he had an air of the great world that one felt in the paper.

As for Albert Nock himself, who was not known at the time

as the highly original essayist he became later, he was a man
of mystery who lived behind a mask or, rather, an iron curtain
of his own devising. Only a few dim facts emerged out of his
heavily shrouded past: he had been an Episcopalian clergyman,
a well-known baseball player and a European emissary of the
State Department. No one knew even where he lived, and a
pleasantry in the office was that one could reach him by placing
a letter under a certain rock in Central Park. He seemed
pathologically reticent, and I remember in one of his essays
a denunciation of obituaries,—he said that "to post a man's
death before the idle newspaper reader" could only be described as "gratuitously filthy." For he hated the notion of what
he called an "unhidden, naked life, without savour or depth,
always on duty to the public." Publicity in any form was
abhorrent to him, and this had quixotic results that were sometimes absurd but that one had to admire, at the same time, also.
If he had, for instance, an article to publish by someone whose
name was in the news, like Maxim Gorky or Constance Markiewicz,—one whom an ordinary editor would have made the
most of,—Nock would cause the article to be printed in extra-
small type with the signature "C. Markiewicz" or "M. Gorky."
He altered the signature of an article by Bernard Shaw so that
"George B. Shaw" appeared as the author. In his peculiar reaction against the usual methods of editors, Nock resembled
Stieglitz as a picture-dealer; for Stieglitz said he was not a
dealer, his gallery was not a gallery and the pictures at his
not-exhibitions were not for sale. In the same way Nock
might have said that *The Freeman* was not a magazine, he was
not an editor himself and his writers were not writers.

In short, with his testy and obstinate look of a Tintoretto
doge, he might have taken for his motto "Hide thy life," and
he was full of surprises in consequence of this,—one never

knew what might turn up in his thought or speech. A Stoic and a crank at once, as well as an Epicurean, he was a formidable scholar and an amateur of music who remembered all the great singers of his day and could trace them through this part or that from Naples to St. Petersburg, London, Brussels and Vienna. He had known all the great orchestras from Turin to Chicago, "as much a participant," he wrote, "as the first violin"; and he had visited half the universities of Europe from Bonn to Bordeaux, Montpellier, Liége and Ghent. He could pick up at random, with a casual air, almost any point and trace it from Plato through Scaliger to Montaigne or Erasmus, and I can cite chapter and verse for saying that whether in Latin or Greek he could quote any author in reply to any question. I believe he knew as well the Old Testament in Hebrew, with many another residuum of his training for orders, for, along with Mr. Dooley, he liked to quote Jeremy Taylor and other old Anglican churchmen like Wilson and Whichcote. A diligently forgotten learning is the mother of culture, he once remarked, but he seemed to have remembered everything, and, besides reading Russian and Spanish with the more usual languages, he had studied Walloon when he was living in Belgium. For the rest, he entered the room at editorial meetings with "the high step and arched back of feline circumspection," his phrase for Jefferson in the salon of Madame de Staël,—Jefferson in whom he saw himself as "the most approachable of men" who was also "the most impenetrable." Idolizing Jefferson, he rather conducted these meetings in the fashion of Lincoln, who had also been a lover of Artemus Ward. As Lincoln transacted the nation's affairs with anecdotes of bears and hogs, tales of frontier circuits and the wisdom of the border, so Nock made his points at meetings of *The Free-*

*man* with references to Rabelais or with homely old American country saws.

It was Nock's wish that *The Freeman* should be an Abbey of Thelema, and his motto for us all was "Do what you like," for he hoped to realize the old humanists' dream of a human association existing in a state of absolute freedom. He was convinced that freedom was the only principle that had never been tried; he saw it as the basis of Henry George's doctrine; and saying, "I am not what Sam Weller called one of the 'advice-gratis' order," he encouraged all the editors to ride their hobbies. For two years, in the last page of the paper, I spoke up for socialism with never a word from Nock that this doctrine was abhorrent to the species of anarchist that he was himself, opposed to all state control and even politics of any kind, as a reader could see at once in the front pages of the paper. But really, concerned for education and the quality of the national mind, Nock had no practical regard for economic matters, and he actually despised Henry George's party. The theory was one thing, but he would never have stirred a finger to put this theory into operation, and he felt that the prophet himself was a fool for thinking political action could ever be an instrument for social improvement. For when "people are incapable of managing even the bad economic system they have, would it not be utter lunacy to entrust them with a good one?" Nock was to remark in *A Journal of These Days,* a question that showed clearly enough how perverse he was or, perhaps one should say, how inconsistent. For how can anyone advocate the measure of freedom that Nock desired unless he believes that people can be trusted with it? Obviously, Nock wished to have it both ways. He revered Jefferson and Henry George, whose doctrines were based on a belief that men are generally born good and educable, while he was more and more convinced that men were generally knaves or fools, ineducable "psychical anthropoids," as Mencken might have put it. For with his good friend Mencken he was largely in agreement.

Of course Nock was quite aware of the shift in his own philosophical base,—which manifested itself in his writings later,—but he was rather puzzling in the days of *The Freeman,* when it seemed to me that he was facing both ways. He was evidently ceasing to believe in the doctrines of the Enlightenment while he clung to his faith in the prophet of San Francisco, and he had as much contempt as Mencken for reformers, uplifters and "settlement sharks," saying that "the state of our society is beyond hope of improvement." He was to observe in his *Memoirs of a Superfluous Man* that he had "gone over to the opposition with head unbowed and withers still unwrung," parting company with Jefferson, Rousseau and Condorcet, while he still disliked "anti-republican nostrums" because "at least provisionally" he thought people sufficiently improvable to sustain republics. But enough! Perverse as he may have been, Nock was somehow tonic, and his repose and distinction of style pervaded, from end to end, a paper that was generally known as the best written in the country. What he called, moreover, his "horror of every attempt to change anybody," or even to "wish to change anybody," meant that he relished the element of character in others just as it was; and, whether the mass of men are or are not educable, his notions of education were good for the few. One could not have called him a lover of his fellow men, but he was undoubtedly humane in his fatalistic fashion, for he felt that poor blundering humankind was really doing the best it could, so why despond or censure anybody? He was actually concerned himself only for the remnant.

I think now of Albert Nock as like one of those Persians or
Chinese whom the eighteenth-century Goldsmith and Mon-
tesquieu imagined,—Usbek, for example, of the *Lettres Per-
sanes*,—visitors to their own native lands from some Asiatic
Utopia where everything was quite different and a great deal
better. Nock's virtual Utopia was Belgium, "the country where
I make my home," as he called it in his *Journal of Forgotten
Days*, and for which, when he was away from it, he felt "the
nostalgia that one is supposed to feel for one's native land."
Why Belgium or, for a city, Brussels?—except that he found
there "the most intelligently presented opera" he knew, and
he never forgot that all Europe had once been indebted to the
Low Countries for the gift of music. I think he had emerged
from Brussels for the four years of *The Freeman* and that he
went back to Brussels when *The Freeman* perished. But he
had other haunts abroad, Luxembourg and Portugal, where
he was to write at least one of his books, and another was
Touraine, the province he described in his engaging *Journey
into Rabelais's Country*. A professional exile, a homeless man,
Nock was a scholar-gypsy, resembling the two friends of his
own youth who had given him "the curious impression of
somehow not belonging where they were." He had always
felt in America like a displaced person,—"like a man who had
landed in Greenland with a cargo of straw hats" and who
found no market for his line of goods there, for it seemed to
him that happiness there was built up of purchasable things
so that he could only feel alone in spirit. He was fond of one
county in Rhode Island where character survived in a stand-
ardized world and where cookery remained an honoured art.
But the characteristic American note was a preference for *doing*, not for the *being* or *becoming* that meant everything to

him, and the humanist was distinctly out of the picture. Nock could only retire within himself.

In much of this he might have been thought another Henry Adams, a No-sayer driven into silence by a chorus of Yeas, and I recalled Adams when I read Nock's wish to be buried on the island of Port Cros, off the French coast, "alone with my recollections." He too disliked what he called the brag, bounce and quackery of our civilization, while he knew as little as Henry Adams of the younger writers of his time unless they happened to be his own personal friends. He was scarcely aware at all of the so-called literary renaissance of which *The Freeman* was obviously one of the symbols; and with a certain disgruntled self-consequence he ignored "on principle" contemporary authors and their work. I would even say that he wrote his *Mont-Saint-Michel and Chartres* in the book, *Francis Rabelais: the Man and His Work*, for in this he too defined his best-beloved human type and the epoch in which he would have felt at home. If, regarding his actual time, he quoted Jefferson's casual guess that the other planets used this one as a lunatic asylum, he loved to think of a day when humanists flourished and among them Rabelais, one of the greatest of all. Rabelais for him was the natural affinity of those who in any time resist or elude all pressure to conform, to accept what they believe to be inhumane, and he felt that the reader developed a like superiority by keeping in touch with a writer who was so joyous and so wise. This was Nock's best work, unless one excepts a few essays and his *Theory of Education in the United States*, defining the humane life and, in its interest, contrasting instrumental and formative education. He meant by the latter education for character and intellect, for what a person can *become* or *be*, while instrumental education meant training for proficiency and bore upon what a person can *do* or *get*. Nock distinguished the kind of man produced by universities such as the plain modest Poitiers and our own, which for him were merely training schools, and, feeling that educable people were as rare as their value to society was great, he would have been happy to see the real thing here.

Nothing in a country mattered to Nock except the quality of its life,—for him banks, telephones and railroads only counted in so far as they contributed to this; and it was his insistence on the question of improving our quality of life that made *The Freeman* so exciting. He was always repeating that this is not Murdstone's world, that it is not fundamentally a place to work in but what Murdstone called a place to mope in,—in other words, a world to be enjoyed; and, meanwhile, as Neilson said, he was a master-craftsman and an exacting lover of good prose. Partly for these reasons Arthur Symons, who sent us many essays, wrote to me that the paper interested him "vastly," while the new writer Malcolm Cowley relished the "agreeably acrid taste" that he found in many of our reviews. Beside them, in its reviews, he felt, *The Nation* tended to be "pompous," *The New Republic* "economic" and *The Dial* "arty." As I was in charge of these reviews, I found it all too easy to send a good many books to English reviewers, for they were so competent, as a rule, in contrast to our own that one could dispatch their copy straight off to the printer. But I soon saw that this would never do. We had to build up a staff of American reviewers, though this meant virtually double work for me. When I had spent afternoons ironing out the gaucheries of eminent fellow-countrymen who were often professors, I began to see how right Nock was in preferring "formative" education to our own generally American "instrumental." It was obvious that formative teaching taught one to write.

As it had been on *The Seven Arts,* so I first met on *The Freeman* a number of good writers who became my friends, among them Malcolm Cowley when he returned from France after spending two years among the Dadaists. I had first heard his name when John Brooks Wheelwright, who had known him there, spoke to me somewhat mysteriously of "Burke and Cowley," not Edmund Burke and Abraham Cowley, as it slowly dawned on me, but the two white hopes of his own generation. One was Malcolm Cowley, one was Kenneth Burke, and they were among the scores of Americans who had printed their essays or poems, or, in several cases, magazines in Europe. Malcolm had printed there, in a blue-covered pamphlet, a fine long essay on Racine that we reprinted. Then there was Matthew Josephson, who had returned with *Secession,* which he carried on in Greenwich Village, and my older friends Walter Pach and Daniel Gregory Mason, who kept us constantly in touch with painting and music. Jack Wheelwright had begun to write a history of American architecture. Veblen and Charles Beard wrote for us, and for a while John Macy, of *The Spirit of American Literature,* was a member of our staff; nor should one forget John Gould Fletcher and Newton Arvin, who was soon to produce fine studies of Melville and Hawthorne. John Dos Passos gave us *Rosinante to the Road Again.* Dos Passos had returned from a postwar visit to Spain, and one gathered that he had been glad enough to escape from the tumult of Europe and the feverish world he had to face at home. For, like Waldo Frank, he saw Spain as somehow outside Europe, a land where life was still a kind of dream, and no doubt it intensified greatly by contrast his impressions of the scene with which he was to deal in *The Big Money.* In Spain he discovered Pio Baroja, whose acute sense of reality must have contributed to the making of *Man-*

*hattan Transfer.* Dos Passos felt that the United States needed acrid writing in order to affect a national mind in which a run-down puritanism was mingled with the ideals of the man in a swivel-chair.

Well I remember Dos Passos in the office of *The Freeman.* His tonsured head,—as it appeared,—was always bent forward, so that, with a sort of Jesuit air of elegant supplication, he suggested a Portuguese saint in a stained glass window. Then I remember too a certain afternoon when Edmund Wilson on the telephone shook my nerves, scolding me for altering the title of his review of some poems of Yeats, an enormity for which I personally was scarcely to blame. There had been a misunderstanding and the change had been made in my absence, though I have no doubt that Wilson was rightly indignant. But in thirty years I have not forgotten the demoralizing onset of that nervously furious presence at the end of the wire. It was a wintry afternoon and I felt like a traveller lost in the snow, beset by a frantic pack of Russian wolves. Yet I admired Wilson as a writer immensely, if only because he ignored that bugaboo of a later time, mass-culture as a deterrent of good writing. He seemed to be always in rapport with a cultivated public, and he found this all the more readily by assuming its existence, a general characteristic of writers for *The Freeman.* The tone of the paper was that of the rigorous amateur, the unspecialized non-professional man of letters; and all our reviews seemed to be written for the interest and pleasure of writing them, not for the mere satisfaction of getting them done.

It was in our office that I met Vernon Parrington, who told me about his *Main Currents of American Thought* and showed me at least some of the earlier chapters. I was perhaps the first person in New York to see them, and later, when I spent a year in the office of Harcourt, Brace and Co., he sent me the first two volumes, which Harcourt published. It was a work that seems typical now of an aspect of the twenties when, as Hendrik van Loon said, economics was in the air and one could not get away from it. Parrington was one of the Nekton who came to *The Freeman*,—to borrow an ichthyological term for fishes possessing a will of their own that takes them across tides and currents. These were of course outnumbered by the literary Plankton, the aimless, directionless drifters, and, along with them, there were the Jellies of whom William Beebe also writes. The Jellies came floating down the tide, as this author puts it, like an endless procession of pale moons.

As for the Nekton, two of these were Henry B. Fuller, the novelist, and Edwin Muir, who wrote to me from London, a writer whom I never met, in spite of our long correspondence, and although we published scores of his essays and reviews. He was A. R. Orage's assistant on *The New Age,* and it was Mencken who brought us together after introducing Muir's first book, in which this writer appeared as a Scottish Zarathustra. An aphorist in the Nietzschean line, with a dry style and a nimble wit, a philosophic farmer's son from the northern islands, Muir, a psychologist who thought in flashes and who believed in the plasticity of man, was bent on giving the race a new direction. As against the complacent and amiable, he was eager for the world to regain the clean, fresh, hardy, innocent spirit of the Greeks, and he saw it as the task of poets and artists not to idealize the origin of man, as writers had done in the past, but to idealize his goal. He pointed out that the great literary myths of the last hundred years,—Faust, Brand, Peer Gynt, Zarathustra,—had all been forecasts of the future, and his touchstone was the elevation of the type man. All this brings back the still hopeful note of a time when the future existed, before the anti-Utopias began to appear. Muir's epigrams had no meretricious glitter but were luminous with the sober light of truth.

Muir, who delighted both Nock and myself, wrote to us presently from Prague, which he found far more stimulating than post-war London, for everything seemed alive to him in the new Czech republic, where there was none of the "heavy English feeling." His own country had seemed to him "terribly dead," while in Prague he found enthusiasm and a light dry air that was almost intoxicating, an atmosphere that was ideal for intellectual work. It had been all but unheard of for an English writer to live in Prague, and it was there, delightfully welcomed by the Czech writers of the twenties, that he began to translate Kafka. Many years later I wondered if Muir's impressions of Czechoslovakia, varied as they were, ample and fresh, would not always be remembered as pictures of that lost republic.

An actual presence at *The Freeman* was Henry B. Fuller, the "father of American realism," as Dreiser called him, who had survived the limbo of the eighteen-eighties. Mencken was astonished to hear that he was still living, and Fuller told me that he was distressed to find himself talked about again as a result of the articles he wrote for our paper. "I have left novel-writing quite behind," he said. "It would be so agreeable to be let alone!" Yet he had only recently published two brief novels, and Randolph Bourne, always alert for anything that was both good and new, had been struck by his *On the Stairs* and *Not on the Screen*. Every book that Fuller produced was an original undertaking, for he broke all his moulds when he had once used them, and these were remarkable experiments in fiction, one showing the value of brevity and one exploring for the novel the technique of the movies. For us he appeared as a man of letters with essays, both scholarly and full of grace, on Beaumarchais and Molière, Dante and Erasmus. The printer might have worked directly from his fine clear script. Fuller was always in my mind when I thought of the prodigal fashion in which mother-ant America forgets its offspring.

## CHAPTER V

# FROM IRELAND

A FEW DOORS from *The Freeman*, on West Thirteenth Street, another old red-brick building housed *The Dial*, the "freely experimental" magazine, a transfiguration of the fortnightly that had been brought from Chicago some years before. Devoted now wholly to literature and art, it stood for everything modern and new at a time when these words still had a mystical meaning, when it might have been said of the literary world that, like the economic world, it had left the gold standard high and dry. For custom and tradition were in process of being turned inside out, they were being pulled apart and torn to pieces, and only good taste unified the contents of *The Dial*, a miscellany of the new writers and graphic artists. I remember once dining there with A. R. Orage, who had published one of my papers in *The New Age*, that model of high thinking and plain living on salaries of, at most, three pounds a week. The apostle of Gurdjieff to the Americans was an odd combination of an eighteenth-century Johnsonian and a mystic of our day.

Between *The Dial* and *The Freeman* there was no great love lost, for Nock was something more than anti-aesthetic and the editors of *The Dial* were aesthetic or nothing; but some of my friends went back and forth as contributors to both, among them Lewis Mumford and Llewelyn Powys. These two writers for *The Freeman* found wives on *The Dial,* for Llewelyn Powys presently married Alyse Gregory, the editor-in-chief, and Lewis married Sophy, who was her assistant. I thought of Lewis and Sophy Mumford as a new Adam and Eve, with whom the human race might well have started, for one could scarcely have imagined a handsomer pair. I always felt as if they had just stepped out of Utopia and were looking for some of their countrymen, astray on this planet, who were also waiting to get back home again. Paul Rosenfeld was the music critic of *The Dial,* and one met in his rooms in Irving Place virtually all the contributors from Zorach to Alfred Kreymborg and William Carlos Williams. There one saw E. E. Cummings, the last of the Yankee come-outers, who came out all the way in his poetry and drawings, and I remember Marianne Moore, on the long sofa by the fire, reading aloud some of her early poems. The mantel and the walls were covered with Marins, Doves, Hartleys and O'Keeffes. One evening Leo Ornstein removed the lid of the piano and smote the keys so violently that he shook these pictures, expressing for Paul, at least, the convulsive activity of the age of steel and the sharp griefs and sharper joys of youth. Paul, who disliked jazz, greatly admired this East Side boy, this mirror held up to the world of the modern city. But, like Huneker, he felt that he had to "get off somewhere," and I think he never liked at all the abstract painting of Mondriaan or the later Schönberg's frigid wastes.

While I cannot recall Llewelyn Powys at any of Paul's evenings, these two were inevitably friends, unlike as they were, the genial urban music-lover and the hardy wiry Dorset man, so redolent of the grass-grown lanes of his native England. During the first years of what he called "starving myself into success" when, fresh from an African sheep-ranch, he was writing for *The Freeman,* he slept on a roof in Patchen Place, ignoring the rain, indifferent to snow, carrying up his blankets through a trap-door. Always living dangerously, setting at nought the tuberculosis that was to kill him so early, he slept in England, when he went home, in a shelter in the fog of the downs, while, as he wrote to me, "the cold wind 'huffled' through the gorse, crying, 'Woe, woe, woe!'" I thought Llewelyn was half in love with death, as only a man can be who loves life fiercely. He was at home in the open, in town or country, sitting, in Switzerland, towards the last, on fallen logs and water-troughs or perhaps in the stables of the peasants. He loved the smell of the cattle-dung as much as the odour of baking bread, while at night he listened to the lonely sound of a trotting horse on the Alpine road outside. I had seen much of him earlier, before he left America, when he said he could live on bread and water-cress. He loved streams, old stone walls and country roads, like the Wolf Pit road in Westport where he and Alyse often appeared on one of their Connecticut excursions. They would pass the pond near our house where "old Paul," as Llewelyn wrote, "lolled like a woodchuck in the sun," and he himself sometimes wore over his shoulders the all but historic plaid shawl that had once belonged to "Omar Khayyám" FitzGerald. Then the two turned in at our garden gate. There was always some sprig of a flowering bush in Llewelyn's shaggy jacket and a knot of wild flowers in his hand.

Never was the style so much the man, for his old-country looks and ways were all of a piece with his naturally antique prose, as full of rural images as the poetry of Herrick, with some of the verbal magic of earlier writers. For, as he liked to think of shepherds and people who measure the passing of the months by the growth of animals and plants, so he was drawn to literary worthies who had been countrymen also, herbalists, gardeners, lovers of meadows and rivers. They too had lived in the senses out of which, for him, had sprung the Dionysian exultation that he was to celebrate in many of his books, the "state of wonder and gratitude" that he called religion and that he was able to match with a splendour of words.

A very different sort of man was the Anglo-Irish Ernest Boyd, although this acidulous Orangeman with the well-combed silky red-brown beard was also an editor's delight. For, as a literary journeyman, by no means an artist or poet in prose, he was always lucid, learned and thoroughly equipped. A linguist, ferociously accurate, a terror to bungling translators and to pseudo-scholars and other half-baked minds, he con-stantly recalled to me the literary gladiators of the Grub Street of the age of Pope and Swift. Boyd's cold eye was death to all pretenders. An impenitent rationalist,—his own phrase,—some-what emotionless and dry, he was more or less versed in the ten literatures of which he wrote studies, and his mind was a copious arsenal of well-digested facts. A biographer of Maupas-sant, whom he translated, and a lover of Anatole France, Boyd had been rather over-impressed by Mencken, and he liked to lay about him with a literary big stick, debunking and hero-baiting in the mood of the moment. It pleased him to make short work of the idols of others, whether Milton or "Aesthete —Model 1924." As the British consul in Copenhagen he had seen much of Georg Brandes, who had deprovincialized Den-mark by introducing the great foreign devils of his time, and he had found Brandes reading Mencken with whom he him-self fell in when the consular service took him to Baltimore. Delighting in Mencken's Rabelaisian armoury of epithets,— smut-hounds, literary pallbearers, boy-snouts and so on,—he had straightway followed this other and lesser man-at-arms of

letters who was deprovincializing America in a similar fashion. But the best of Boyd came out when he wrote of his own
countrymen as a critic and historian of the Irish literary movement. His *Appreciations and Depreciations,* published in Dublin in 1918, a collection of sensitive essays on the writers of
this movement, had been for me a treasure of the time.

I had had some correspondence with Boyd before he came to
the United States, and at first sight he suggested at once another brown-bearded Orangeman whom I had known in New
York some years before. This was at Petitpas', in the company
of John Butler Yeats, and the learned man I mean was the
Sanskritist Charles Johnston, who had been an early friend of
Yeats the poet. With his vaguely Presbyterian look and a
chilliness like Boyd's, austere and even majestic, as I recall him,
Charles Johnston had founded in Dublin the Hermetic Society, one of the principal springs of the Irish revival. It had
been a great part of the "Celtic wave" that had not yet been
discredited by Joyce with his contemptuous reference to the
"cultic twalette," a movement that had fascinated me ever
since my college days and led me to sit at the feet of the grand
old Yeats. In the hundreds of hours I spent with him at Petitpas', out in the country, at my own house, in the houses of
some of our friends, I felt that I had lived at least within
sight of AE, George Moore, John Eglinton, W. B. Yeats and
Lady Gregory. For "J.B." had witnessed the whole movement,
and of this, as Boyd remarked, one had a complete iconography
in his pencil drawings and larger portraits. At any moment,
as he talked, he would sketch for me George Moore or Synge
to illustrate some point of character that amused him, and I
can see now that I was greatly influenced by this, conscious
as I was of our own parallel movement.

Two other figures of the Irish revival who were living in

New York and of whom I saw much in years to come were
Padraic Colum, who breathed and spread an atmosphere of
poetry, and his wife Mary,—Mollie,—who wrote for *The Freeman*. Of the young authors of the Irish theatre Padraic was
the first to be produced, and he had inaugurated with Synge,
a few weeks later, the drama of Irish peasant life. Then, writing mainly dramatic lyrics, he was drawn to the heroic age of
Greece, as later the legends of Hawaii attracted him also. In
*The Golden Fleece* and *The Adventures of Ulysses* he retold,
in lovely prose, tales of great warriors and chiefs who had
something in common with the semi-mythical heroes of his own
country, while Mollie, brought up in the west of Ireland, was
born to love poetry too in a world of strolling musicians and
ballad-singers. She had heard rumours there as a girl of the
poets and playwrights in Dublin whose characters were the
people she knew well,—fiddlers, beggar women on the roads,
—and she presently found herself, at the National University,
"stepping right into the Irish revival." She was to recall in *Life
and the Dream* the days when the names of Yeats and Synge,
magical names, appeared on the Dublin billboards and these
great men had begun to replace with writings about their own
land the English themes of Tennyson, Meredith and Swinburne. As she saw, the language movement and the literary
movement gave the Irish good heart for other matters, awakening in everyone the longing for a national literature and life,
dispelling the defeatist spirit of the provincial past.

In Dublin, as a student, she had idolized the poet Yeats,
who excited all the susceptible young men and women, so that
they followed him through the streets and watched him, sunk
in dream, while his lips moved rhythmically as if he were com-
posing. They liked to think that he was weaving magic spells
in what seemed to be a walking trance, and at their various

clubs he talked about poetry and criticism, as I heard him talk on his first visit to this country. Well I remember him in his black jacket and flowing tie, with his hair over his eyes, as in Sargent's drawing, and I could guess how moving all this must have been to students after long days in Dublin classrooms. Mollie Colum brought back too the tenseness in the air when *The Playboy of the Western World* was first produced and a riot broke out in the theatre, and she had been present at George Moore's lecture on the French impressionists and regularly at AE's famous evenings. There all the talk was of literature and art and the ways in which novels and plays were written, with good practitioners eager to expose their methods and with the great-hearted AE leading the talk. Constantly present in the Dublin scene was the romantic Maud Gonne, the heroine of the revolutionary movement whom I was to see later.

One could imagine Mollie herself, with her slender figure and wild red hair,—she had "come from the country of Isolde," as Richard Strauss remarked,—in the Dublin of a time when everyone seemed to be young and all things seemed to be beginning. The young ran everything, especially the schools of Padraic Pearse in one of which Mollie was a teacher, and imagination and devotion were the notes of the moment, a general dedication to one cause or another. Yeats, impressed by her reviews and saying she had talent as a critic, advised her to become an authority in some literary field, perhaps the French literature that interested her deeply, just as it interested the American writers who had turned away from England to France and Russia. For the sake of their independence they had been obliged to escape from the overwhelming influence of the old mother-country. As a critic Mollie had rare qualifications, for, trained severely as she was in literary scholarship, she was an active participant in a movement of the present, in a small capital city in ferment, as Boston had been once, so that practice and theory were equally vivid to her. Yeats himself had made a cult of discipline, and Mollie had undergone the strict harsh mediæval drill that Joyce described in the "portrait" of his own upbringing. She had taken the same courses and the same degree as Joyce, and, understanding intuitively the writers whom she met, she was well versed in the art of literary living.

I was to profit by this myself in the days of *The Freeman* and afterwards, for, while no one hated more than Mollie anything woolly in thought or style, few were as practically wise in literary matters. She was aware that unsuitable people could wreck a writer's talent, as one saw every day in promiscuous New York, in the atmosphere of Greenwich Village parties, and she had a fine feeling for the enchantment of words and a fierce and rigorous truthfulness, together with the gifts of intensity and accurate perception. No one knew better the difference between real writers and dilettanti or the "highly intelligent commonplace" creators for the market, those who supported the powerful fiction-producing industry whom she described later in *From These Roots*. She detested the decadent realism, the concentration on the exterior life that discredited the interior life in contemporary writing, the flat impoverished materialist philosophy that tended to destroy every expression in words of the life of dream. In her reviews in *The Freeman* she defended from all assaults the writers who were devoted to a true vocation, and, struck by the prestige of English opinion in our still colonial New York, she understood our "nationalist" feeling here. She realized that our problems were somewhat like those she had known at home, and she saw why the Irish revival had so interested me.

For, at a period when I felt so strongly that American literature was coming of age, I could scarcely not have been struck by this earlier movement, when another literary dependency of England was finding its own character and asserting its own national culture, in the phrase of the moment. When later I saw myself accused of cultural flag-waving and chauvinism,—and even of a narrow nationalism,—I realized how remote nowadays had become a point of view that was generally current in the days of which I am writing. I mean it was current in many minds of the "new" literary countries in which an indigenous literature was fairly recent, even in Ibsen's Norway and Dostoievsky's Russia whose literary history was, in a way, still nascent. It might never have occurred to a Frenchman to say what Ibsen said, "Culture is unthinkable apart from national life," and no Englishman need ever have been afraid of losing his Englishness as Dostoievsky was afraid of becoming "less Russian." But when nations are establishing their own cultural autonomy, escaping from outside influences that have annulled this in the past, they are obliged to reject these influences that have overborne them,—how otherwise can they assert their collective selfness? Ireland required the "De-Anglicization" that Douglas Hyde called for precisely at the moment when Yeats was affirming, "There is no fine literature without nationality. You can no more have the greater poetry without a nation than religion without symbols." Whether in writing to Katharine Tynan or in his *Letters to the New Island,* Yeats repeated this over and over, aware as he was necessarily that this idea might be used not to expand but to narrow the horizon of the mind. It was a matter of both time and degree, and at the time he was also aware that the Irish writers had taken too much from English traditions and literature at the expense of their own. It was just when

George Moore's dæmon said to him, "Go to Ireland" that Yeats summoned Synge back from Paris, begging him to steep himself in Irish folklore. He said, "We peer over the wall at our neighbour's garden instead of making our own garden green and beautiful. And yet it is a good garden and there have been great transactions within it."

That we too required "De-Anglicization" Mencken, for one, had clearly seen, although he had never put it in quite this fashion,—he was rather moved by a German racial bias; and was it not evident that, for the moment at least, we had to believe in cultural nationalism also? As for this, English writers especially had always looked down on our literature because it was colonial and imitative, because it lacked raciness, a native autochthonous quality, because our writers were too much like their own. They had always asked us to be ourselves, regretting that we were not, for all our declarations of independence, and this general complaint of the English from the time of Bryant and Irving down had been expressly repeated by Emerson and Whitman. It interested me that in the world of painting the French critics praised John Sloan because he was so different from their own painters, ignoring others, technically abler, who reflected Paris, precisely because Sloan was steeped in his American scene. So I could not understand why I was accused of chauvinism when political nationalism meant to me so little, when I would have been glad to surrender sovereignty, with all the other nations, for the sake of world unity and understanding. I was not preaching America *über alles* or any such nonsense. Cultural identity was all that ever interested me, while the actual America of my belief was the nation of its promise, a nation that too often broke its word. For the rest, in those earlier days, I was stirred by Mazzini and his idea of the function of nations as the workshops of humanity, each with a peculiar gift to contribute to the whole. Mazzini saw humanity as a great army marching to the conquest of unknown lands, and he thought of the peoples as its corps, each with a special duty to perform and a special operation to carry out. Each nation therefore must needs be seen as a living homogeneous entity with its own faith and consciousness of self,—or so, at least, I understood this great man who possessed my mind, with Whitman, Ibsen, Nietzsche and half a dozen others.

Of these one was AE, whose book *The National Being* I somehow connected with Mazzini, for it invoked a national purpose and a literature expressing this along the lines of its own racial genius. For my own effort to put into words a similar thought I must have been indebted to AE, as I was certainly indebted to him for coming to feel that Emerson was the "fountain-head" or "germ-cell" of our culture. I am quoting from the letters I received from that man, "passionately good,"—in the phrase of Unamuno,—to whom even the incredulous Boyd was whole-heartedly devoted. First or last, in *The Irish Homestead* or *The Irish Statesman*, AE reviewed five of my books; and, although I never saw him, I took him for an oracle as, for years, I had taken J. B. Yeats. He was not the only Irishman who loved our great writers. It had not escaped me that Standish O'Grady, whose bardic history of Ireland was the first cause perhaps of the Irish revival, had sung in early days the praises of Whitman; and there was John Eglinton,—Magee,—the "lonely thorn-tree" that "breaks into flower," as, in *Hail and Farewell*, George Moore called him. I could never forget the excitement with which, in the New York Public Library, I read *Two Essays on the Remnant* and *Pebbles from a Brook*, discovering the beautiful essayist for whom, in his own youth, Emerson and Thoreau had meant more than any other writers. ("With the possible exception of Wordsworth," he wrote to me later. "At one time I almost seemed to live their lives. You saw where I came from, mentally and spiritually.") This so-called "Irish Emerson" also affected my point of view as, more and more, I came to feel that Emerson, Thoreau and Whitman were creators of our one indigenous tradition of the spirit. But AE especially led me to see what I had not seen in America at the time when I wrote *America's Coming-of-Age*, and, although I was never satisfied with the *Life of Emerson* that followed this, I owed to him largely the wish to write it.

I had wonderful letters from AE, usually opening with a pastel sketch of trees, supernatural figures, the rim of a lake, sometimes written from Donegal and the whitewashed cottage he had there in which his happiest days, he said, were spent. The cottage was set amid mountains, miles from anywhere in the world, overlooking rocky islets and silvery beaches, and there on one of his visits he had brought nothing to read but a twelve-volume translation of the Mahabarata. He encountered there by chance a man who read Indian philosophy and talked with him one morning for an hour, an instance of what he called Emerson's law of spiritual gravitation, which brings together those who are intended to meet. He had first met Yeats, he said, seemingly by accident, he had talked with Shaw two hours without knowing who he was, and he had chanced to fall in with Charles Johnston, the translator of the Sacred Books of the East, just after he had first found these books himself. Always knowing that he could not miss the people who rightly belonged to him, he had never tried to meet anyone or sought anyone out; for he felt that forestalling the law was like plucking apples before they are ripe and the relations that followed were never satisfying.

In one letter he took me to task for overrating Swinburne, one of our literary heroes when I was in college, saying he could never have rivalled Blake's gift of making lines that were "like flowers of sound carved out of the air." Nature, he added, had given Swinburne "an interminably long family of words to bring up and an insufficient income of ideas to support them on." Then he dwelt on the subject of poverty and its importance to literary men, a theme that interested many in my generation. For, in reaction as we were against the idea of success and the whole character of a business civilization, we were attracted to failure, so called, to the misfits of E. A. Robinson's world and to poverty as one of the marks of this. "Talent doesn't starve any more," said one of Scott Fitzgerald's men, anticipating the remark of a later writer that "the attic is no place to evolve ideas," but William James felt otherwise when he agreed with Thoreau that poverty and spiritual freedom are not unconnected. When I thought of the "attic" ideas of Paine, of Whitman and of Robinson, in Veblen's world of "pecuniary emulation," I felt that AE must surely be right in his constant recommendation that writers should take the vow of poverty. "All my literary friends are poor," he wrote once, "except Lord Dunsany who was born with an income, and the needs of life are much fewer than people suppose. The two great needs are good talk and plenty of solitude to brood and dig deep. I live now very economically, as my fixed income is about £100 a year, but am I unhappy? Good God, no. Yeats had long years of poverty and never sold his talent. Stephens was living on one pound a week when he wrote *The Crock of Gold*." AE went on, "Writers should stand ready to desert prosperity if it conflicts with the spirit." After his wife's death, when the lights of home were far behind him, he got rid of all his impedimenta, and, keeping only a few shirts and books, as he wrote to me, he felt free to wander like an antique sage.

AE,—George Russell,—was one of those men, like the author of *The Tragic Sense of Life,* who think not only with their brains but with flesh and bone, with their lungs, their hearts and blood, with their whole bodies. No doubt in some ways Gertrude Stein, the oracle of younger men, possessed this rare integrality that makes the seer,—or, in her case, equally, the sibyl,—and she found in Emerson a quality she missed in Hemingway and Faulkner,—in fact, in "all" the new American writers. "Good craftsmen and honest men," they had "passions merely," she remarked in a published conversation, while, as for "passion," they did not have it, though they knew all about it and could sometimes write about it very surely. But, she continued, Emerson, who did not know about it and could not have written about it, really had passion,—words that brought back to me something that AE said apropos of Emerson and our new writers. I doubt if AE knew much about these new writers specifically, or about novelists in general, or the novelist's mind, but he was well up in the America of the past and the present; and he said that the present generation of Americans had "gone from central depths to surfaces" while Emerson himself "went into occult depths."

AE might have said the same thing of *Moby-Dick,* as he actually said it of *Leaves of Grass* and *Walden,* a group of books that in South America and, as I knew, in India were universally regarded as the Scriptures of this country. They expressed the "soul of America," as *The Aryan Path* constantly said, and for me they came to be the standard to which to appeal when I saw the limitations of our actual country. To AE they were the work of planetary minds, and these books had led him to "look to America for the literature and art of the future." My own new serious reading of them completely changed the feeling that I had acquired in college about our old writers. In regard to them I was preparing to write in the twenties what I actually wrote in *Makers and Finders* later.

## CHAPTER VI

# UA TANE

THE NINETEEN-TWENTIES were "an age of islands," Malcolm
Cowley wrote once, when "almost everyone seemed to be
looking for an island," when thousands of Americans fled to
Majorca, Capri, the West Indies and scores sailed away for
the South Seas. They wished to secede from society, they believed in "Secession,"—the name of Matthew Josephson's magazine,—generally in revolt as they were against the bourgeois
world they knew and the values of a business civilization.
Like Melville, three generations before, like Henry Adams in
the eighties, like Charles Warren Stoddard and Lafcadio
Hearn, many were drawn to the primitive life in their wish to
break away from everything that characterized modern living.
They disliked the "duplicity of civilized man" and the "frigid
manners of the Christians," as one of the earlier exiles to
Polynesia put it, and one and all were inclined to say "Blessed
be savagery!"—for them the condition of grace and the true
joy of living.

I had known well this point of view some years before the
twenties because of my brother-in-law John Francis Stimson,
—so named in honour of Jean-François Millet, his artist-father's
idol,—who had gone out to Tahiti in 1912. He had been attracted to the South Seas after reading *Typee* and *Omoo* in
my house at Palo Alto, when I was teaching there at Stanford

University and Frank was an architect in San Francisco. Formerly a draughtsman of Stanford White, he had studied in Paris at the Beaux-Arts and had shown extraordinary promise in architecture; but, unwilling to be second at Rome or in California, he preferred to be a Caesar somewhere else. He had grown up in the Wall Street suburb of my childhood where, with his sister,—my wife,—and Maxwell Perkins, I had known him from kindergarten days; while, packing a world of chequered adventure into his first thirty years, he had concluded that America was simply a "nightmare." With what he called a "powerful bias toward liberty of action and conscience,"— inherited, as he said, from his father, the painter,—he established himself near the spot where his most intimate friends were to live,—the writers Charles Nordhoff and James Norman Hall. During the next forty years, he was to realize, largely at least, his "dream of becoming the world authority on Polynesia," the "genius" of Charles Nordhoff's phrase with a wider knowledge of the islands and their speech than any Polynesian had ever possessed.

Until the first world war broke out, he had a vanilla plantation on the shore of Cook's Bay on the island of Moorea, where he hung up fragments of the chintz curtains from Captain Cook's own cabin that were sent to him from England by the voyager's descendants. Early up and breakfasting on coffee and bananas, he paddled his outrigger canoe to the reef, spearing fish to supplement his usual diet of fruits and swimming in the blue waters of the lagoon there. For the sharks never came inside the arc of foam that indicated the presence of the reef, while fishes of light indigo and emerald green darted about him as he swam over the white sand and among the coral boulders. He was, like all the Tahitians, athletic and brown, though he was exposed to elephantiasis on this "fee-

fee" island, as well as to various fevers and tuberculosis. He found he was eating bread from a bakery where the baker was rotten with leprosy, while he was served for a time by a syphilitic waitress, and the little polyps of the live yellow coral on which he scraped his knee one day got into the flesh of the cut and caused serious trouble. From this came a dreadful sore which he only cured by soaking it for weeks in carbolic acid. The soil of the island was so full of germs that he was obliged to touch every mosquito bite with acid and peroxide. Centipedes, moreover, abounded there and he had neighbours with elephantiasis whose arms occasionally swelled to the size of beer-kegs. But, guided as he felt he was by fate, he threw off all infections, convinced that "something is coming," as he wrote to his mother, "that will be its own explanation and justification." He knew he was there "for a purpose," and, spending several hours a day learning the language of the natives, he began to work for the Mormon missionaries. At first he corrected their sermons, and presently he compiled for them a Tahitian-English dictionary and a Tahitian grammar. His house on the shore looked up to the crest of Mount Rotui with misty peaks rising from the forest, where the rainbows were of pale opalescent hues, ethereal as the vanishing shades in the antique delicate older Japanese prints. He dreamed of a Japanese garden there with little pools and shaded nooks under the great waterfall tumbling over the cliffs; and he drew up plans for a houseboat inside the great reef where he could enjoy a Paul and Virginia existence.

He was full at this time of Lafcadio Hearn, whom he had discovered at Yale, and he saw in Polynesia a vast field like Hearn's Japan waiting for someone properly to treat it. With him it was only a question of the best approach, and his own aesthetic and literary interest was already yielding to scientific interests, linguistic and ethnic. His second great hope was to see no more of the "hell" that America was creating for itself. He seemed to prefer "nature men" to the company of what he called clean-cut Americans on vacation, though he had civilized cronies in the Cercle Bougainville and especially his beloved Nordhoff and Hall. Meanwhile, owing to the first world war and the failure of the vanilla trade, he joined a ship-outfitter's concern in Papeete, a connection he was to retain for several years until he became an associate of the Bishop Museum. His mathematical training helped him with the cost-book, the price-book, the stock-book, the day-book, the journal and the ledger, and he began to feel that he possessed the qualities which made a good South Sea trader. He even indulged in day-dreams of making a fortune that reminded me of Mark Twain's Colonel Sellers, no longer as a vanilla king but by selling concrete tables and chairs to replace the wooden furniture that was devoured by insects. Then he planned to raise hens hygienically, something unheard of on the islands, for the natives let their hens run loose with the result that most of them died from eating mangoes rotting on the ground. But these were mere fantasies beside the vision that filled his mind and that he was beginning to realize almost at the outset. He was already studying a dozen Polynesian dialects six years after his first arrival on the islands.

He had married a French-Tahitian girl whose four brothers had all been drowned in Nordhoff and Hall's "Hurricane" of Hikueru, and he himself was to become, as we saw from time to time, both more and more French and more and more Tahitian. His native name was Ua Tane, pronounced over him by Prince Pomare, the corpulent nephew of the former king whom one saw fishing at the end of the wharf or driving in his frail buggy about the island. Meanwhile, the Gauguinesque quality that was marked in his father's appearance came out very soon in Frank as well. In the little house in which Gauguin had lived only ten years before he arrived, he found a glass door which the artist had painted, and he shared Gauguin's taste for the purple of the Tahitian earth, for the jagged peaks and the orange and scarlet vegetation. He liked the tropical flowers that were ranker and sharper than the American flowers with their pastel shades. Frank's letters, which came every month on the boat that sailed up from New Zealand, abounded in these objects and scenes, with the bougainvilleas that riotously grew and blossomed all the year round and the twenty luscious fruits to be had for plucking them off the trees, together with the climbing vine that bore musk-melons.

There was much talk in his letters too of the squatters on his Moorea land and some of the rascally colonial pettifogging lawyers, along with the psychic adventures and the spirit-conversations in which, with all his nihilism, he had great faith. A fascinated reader of Sir Oliver Dodge and Conan Doyle, he found a competent medium in Papeete, and, sharing Lafcadio Hearn's "scientific mysticism," he often heard and communed with spirit voices. By this means, in fact, he solved the supposedly insoluble problem in chess that was called the "Eight Self-Block Task." Frank found the key, he said, within three hours after the request was given to the "operators" to materialize it; and his triumph was presently celebrated in the chess magazines. But to one who had always known him this was not surprising. I remembered that when we were boys he defeated the turbaned automaton that played chess at the entrance of the Eden Musée in New York, a famous player behind his disguise who was supposed never to have been beaten; and Frank set other world records in special "task" fields. He had, as he said once, "the kind of mind that sees order in complex situations." For the rest, in his letters he sometimes described fishing by lantern light on the reef, or he wrote about the home-grown coffee that one gathered in the morning, roasted in the afternoon and brewed for supper, a supper of sea-centipedes, perhaps, or shrimps. Or he would talk about Nordhoff and Hall, or the Swedish planter whom he liked or Jack London's friend who lived, stark naked, on the mountain. Or one of the broken souls who had arrived in Tahiti.

Then Frank had long talks with the old Queen Marau, the daughter of Arii-taimai whose memoirs had been written by Henry Adams and whose own mind brimmed over with the legends of her childhood. She was the one person in whom was concentrated all the ancient lore of Tahiti. Some time earlier she had sent a servant with a message to the nurse that she wished Frank to call upon her, but, having got up, as he put it, on the wrong side of the bed that day, he was annoyed by the manner of this invitation. He sent back word that in his family,—the formidable family he defied at home,—invitations were sent in a different fashion; and, hearing nothing more from her, he supposed the old lady had taken offence at his hoity-toity response to her suggestion. Then her daughter, the Princess Takau, who had heard of his work, intervened, and the queen sent him a courteous invitation. "She spoke," he wrote, "the most beautiful and elevated English and French, and of course her Tahitian is the most perfect now spoken by any living man or woman. It was a delight and pleasure that I cannot express to you. She greatly admired some of my own translations of the old Tahitian poetry." When, later, he read aloud to her, she said to him, "You read these chants as my ancestors would have spoken them." He took the old queen copies of two of his books, and he sent back to America for a flat reading-glass to enable her to read again with pleasure. Meanwhile, he found in Tahiti one youngish man who had memorized some of the legends when he was a boy and was able to recite them still in the stately old language. Frank took them down at his dictation. One of them recounted the story of a Tahitian cannibal king who had learned cannibalism from his foster-parents, proving, as it seemed to Frank, that, for all the belief to the contrary, this had been a practice in Tahiti.

However, from Frank's point of view, Tahiti was too civilized, and it was too much written about as well. He was eager to visit and study the more distant and interesting islands that were scarcely accessible to Europeans, even at present, where he could learn at first hand, from the old men who remembered them, the ways of this disappearing people. He wished to record its traditions, its folk-tales and genealogies, its cosmogonic formulas, chants and prayers, for he was deeply interested in questions of religion as long as they were exotic and picturesque. As the architect of an East Indian bungalow-palace, he had made a study of Buddhism in San Francisco, along with the hermetic philosophy of ancient Egypt; and he wished now to investigate the old Polynesian religion, hoping to find traces of it on some of the islands. His earliest voyages were mere trips on small trading schooners to represent his company in Papeete, visits to the less distant islands to encourage the planting of cocoa and rubber or anything that would make them more productive. He knew the dialect of the Marquesas, distinct from Tahitian, though similar in structure, and he soon made friends with the native chiefs on these high mountainous islands with their well-watered valleys between the ridges. The islands were bold and wild, with great cliffs abutting on the sea, broken off sheer and scooped out with caverns, for there were no barrier reefs to protect them from the waves, and Frank visited Taipi-vai, the great valley that Melville called Typee, and saw old Marquesan dances still performed there. Later, on sloops and copra schooners, or Chinese trading-vessels, with cargoes of arrowroot, coffee and pandanus mats, he was to range far and wide through the South Seas, recalling to my imagination the voyage among the isles of Melville's hero Taji and Jarl the Skyeman. In Frank's letters I overheard the conversation in the Ti as well, and I seemed to be present at the Feast of Calabashes.

From time to time, at Westport, Frank's friends sought us out, one a French pearl-trader and one a German-American artist who had also spent six years in Tahiti. Thence this young man of romantic descent had sailed to Bora-Bora and later, with Frank also, to the Tuamotus, where civilization had reached the point of introducing beds, not to be slept upon but only under. There Ua,—Frank,—at that time working on his Tuomotuan dictionary and regarded as a chief himself, conversed with the sages, along with the local Mohis and Babbalanjas from whom he gathered in fragments the legends of the islands. To his friends there he had brought gifts of banana plants. In the story of his own island life, this German-American artist related how fluent and soft was Frank's Tuamotuan and how canny he was never to sail without aspirin and rum or without inspecting the vessel on which they were sailing. For now and then the owners poured cement inside along the keel, and this so strained the ribs that in a storm the bottom of the schooner sometimes dropped out. South Sea cruising to Frank was already an old story. He knew all the captains and all the schooners, the rotten and the sound, and always slept on a mat on the quarter-deck. At Bora-Bora the two had seen Frank's old friend Matahi,—the hero of *Tabu*, which had been photographed there,—with his great bronze chest, his frangipani garland, his grass skirt and flowers in his hair. Matahi and his troupe danced for them under the palms.

To Westport, too, for several visits, came James Norman Hall, Frank's "best friend in all the world," who turned back to Tahiti once, after setting out to see China and Japan, so homesick he was for his thatched roof on the island. There time, he said, was a serpent with its tail in its mouth, gliding so smoothly in a circle that one was scarcely aware it moved at all. By nature the hermit of a South Sea Walden, Hall shared Thoreau's hatred of cities and banks, but he was the most humane of men, like Robert Flaherty, Frank's other friend, who was for some time our neighbour in New Canaan. I was to see more in later years of this "father of the documentary film" who produced his *Moana of the South Seas* on one of the islands, while he sold out his interest in *Tabu* when he was not permitted to carry out his full intention in it. He had wished to show beyond peradventure how the impact of civilization destroyed the moral fibre of primitive cultures. "Bob" Flaherty had always been looking on the fringes of the world for traces of the heroic life of earlier ages, remnants of the Homeric scene that had long since vanished with what he accepted sadly as the decline of the West. He who might still have been at home in the world of Audubon and Fenimore Cooper loved the Eskimo country and the Aran islands, and he hoped to find in the South Seas the rustic Greece of the golden age that Henry Adams had said was still alive there. He grieved over the decadence, as he called it, of modern writing, the total absence in it of the nobility of Melville, and he had only contempt for a time that could see nothing but Apeneck Sweeneys and Hemingway's killers, bull-fighters and racketeers. Above all other qualities he loved elevation, and, from his point of view, humanity had sunk, in our world war epoch, to a lower level.

At intervals of about ten years, Frank himself reappeared with his ever-increasing look of a Polynesian idol or one of those chieftains, born to command, authoritative and massive, whom Henry Adams pictured in his South Sea letters. For he had the stout "royal body" of the Ariki, the high chiefs and kings, always well nourished and for that reason all the more respected. Once he came up with Nordhoff and Hall, who said that on the steamer he had lectured to the passengers on the wonders of the islands, enthralling them as, in our house, he enthralled young and old, as Melville had enthralled the Hawthornes when they were at Lenox. He had met on some faraway island a native who remembered cannibalism and the joy of munching an enemy's thigh or arm-bone,—or the plump palm of a hand, a special tidbit,—and who murmured wistfully, "O how good it was!" recalling these delights of human flesh. Frank too had practised the ancient art of fire-walking when, with a dozen initiates, on bare feet, he had traversed a trench full of red-hot stones, immune against any burns, because, like the faithful of whom he was one, he never doubted for a moment that he could do so. At the same time he related how quickly those who lost faith and heart leaped from the coals in agony at the first step. Or he would describe the great fish-drive in the Leeward islands when the circling line of canoes approached the white beach, driving the fish before them as the paddlers with great stones attached to long lines brought these down upon the sea with resounding splashes. The frightened fish moved swiftly into the shallows, and there they were speared and caught by long drags of cocoanut fronds to the sound of the speeches and songs of the watching chieftains.

Sometimes he spoke of the travellers who visited Tahiti,—

for one, Lloyd Osbourne, the stepson of Stevenson, who asked
him for copies of his Polynesian chants. He was sure that
Delius, the composer, would set them to music. One day
Vilhjalmur Stefansson arrived on his way up from New Zealand with wonderful tales of his own Arctic adventures in the
land of the blond Eskimos where with his last bullet he had
shot two caribous at once and saved his party. For they had
all been threatened with starvation. Then Henri Matisse
stopped for a week on his journey round the world and Frank
spent days with him driving about the island road, for this
artist wished to avoid all engagements with officials. Matisse
did not share Gauguin's interest in the people of the island
but he seemed to be fascinated by the tropical colours, the
contrast of brown, green and yellow; and, as Robert Flaherty
was there, Frank brought the two together, apparently to the
great delight of both. Matisse could not hear enough about
Flaherty's own work and the way in which he arrived at his
conceptions. Frank had a special feeling for the few great
skippers who were left and who had what he called wide
horizons and what they called untainted winds to breathe,
Andy Thomson of the "Tagua" and Vigo Rasmussen, the
Dane, with both of whom he had sailed on more than one
occasion. Andy, who had brought him a hat from Manihiki,
was a master-navigator in a cyclone, and Vigo Rasmussen of
Raratonga, a recluse with a deep inner life, was the captain of
the most beautiful schooner in all the South Seas. His cabin
in the "Tiare Taporo" was lined with books. Frank had less
respect for some of the native captains who were unable to
find their position in the ocean. Struck by the danger of this
in cruising, he bought a chronometer and sextant and took
lessons in navigation from the Captain of the Port, so that, as

long as he had a sight of the sun, he could find any position anywhere.

Often I urged Frank to write out the story of his adventures, for they seemed to me as unusual as Sir Richard Burton's, but he had no interest in the picturesqueness of his own life and he said he was not a good observer. He was not detached enough for this, he was too close to the Polynesians; and so, as he put it, he missed the bright colours of the surface of their life, while he sought for the warp and woof of its inner texture. He could not in writing revive the local details that came out so fully in his talk. Intensely drawn to the Polynesians, entirely at home with them, he thought, as it seemed to him, actually as they did, and he remembered moonlight nights when, sitting with them on a beach, he felt they were telling stories of his own forbears. Many of them were convinced that he was literally an incarnation of one of their own high priests or ancient nobles, and he rather encouraged this notion, for it made them feel it was useless to withhold any of their secrets from such a man. They concealed nothing from him and related events of their psychic life which they would never have told their Christian pastors. Remembering the previous travellers, from Captain Cook down to the present, he could think of no one who had had his advantages, for the natives never opened their minds entirely to the missionaries and most of the others were commoners from the native point of view. They had usually been sailors or castaways, and these men did not know how the Ariki acted and spoke in the inviolability of their inner circles.

Once Frank brought back with him two cases bulging at the sides with notebooks and other records of Raivavai, many of them written by Hapai, the venerable son of the last high chief of Mahanatoa. Frank had sailed down on a schooner to this Austral island, spending many months there but finding that Hapai had left Raivavai for Tahiti. He had wished to put his grandchildren in school there, while his wife pined for the movies, and the couple had settled near Frank's own house where they lived by making copra, at the same time preparing candied bananas. Hapai, now the deacon of the Protestant chapel, was a not uncommon case of fallen grandeur; for some of the descendants of the heroes of old songs of conquest and love,—masters of their fate,—lived by selling postcards. With the aid of his friend Admiral Byrd, Frank employed Hapai for several years to write out in his own hand the secret teachings of the island with detailed descriptions of the traditional social life, canoe-building, house-building, plaiting, weaving and so on. The old man related how the islanders had built their ovens and fire-pits, manœuvred their fish-sweeps and chipped their stone, and he made plans and drawings of the archery platforms and temple enclosures that were scattered along the beaches or hidden in the valleys. Earlier explorers had known only twenty of these stone-walled temples, while Frank's associate Alan Seabrook found two score and ten with massive upright slabs leaning or fallen. The beautifully tesselated floors had been displaced or broken by the up-thrusting shrubbery or the trunks of trees, and the stone images had been shattered or carried off to fill in the foundation walls of churches. Frank had explored these temples in the silence of the valleys, a pre-European forest world such as John Lloyd Stephens had known a century before in Guatemala.

Raivavai was the scene of some of Frank's most important work. It was a small island where others had found nothing, so that no one supposed any of the old lore was left there. On this great mountain mass the oranges fell to the ground in showers, like a yellow carpet glimmering through the green of the trees,—the lagoon teemed with vari-coloured fishes,—and there one of the sages, who became a friend of Frank's, recorded for him old stories of the island. Frank gave him several notebooks in which he could write his accounts of the ancient Polynesian skippers and their exploits and voyages, and every few days, after filling one of these, Tauira'i walked the length of the island to see him. From others Frank collected songs and genealogies going back to the gods who created the world from a void of black water, with recitations of the royal bards that celebrated demigods and heroes at the great feasts remembered from the past. He examined the scenes of the tournaments or emulative battles in which the youthful warriors had exhibited their prowess. From a throng of canoes in the lagoon the people had watched them. These were the young men who had sailed to Hawaii and New Zealand carrying all before them wherever they went, vikings and sea-rovers like Tapu-ehu who had landed with seventy companions at Raiatea. He had greeted with these words the reigning chief, "I have come to fling your warriors, like so much refuse of the beach, into the sea." The divers in those days plunged ninety feet down into the ocean to seize with their bare hands and a noosed rope a great turtle as large as a dining-room table and bring it up at midnight through the black waters. Other tales were gentler, like some of the chants. The subject of one of these was the great ship of Kihotumu, the ship that sailed the Milky Way and swept across the heavens to anchor in the land of one of the god's eight temples. Another related the return of the ship Marama from a certain long voyage among the isles. The steersman, donning his formal robe of office, watched the clouds on the horizon for the headlands of home, and, as the boat sailed in, the voyagers recognized faces on the shore and danced with joy after the years of separation. When they were assured of a friendly welcome, the leader unwrapped the figures of the gods they had carried with them as safeguards against shipwreck and storms, and then he pretended to dry the crimson plumes, his insignia of rank, that were supposed to have been wet by the spray. Not till then did the company venture to land.

Like the great Anaa series of archaic legends, these chants revealed fleeting glimpses of a prehistoric past, a high civilization that had utterly vanished; and Frank could only feel that, if he had not been there, this would have left behind no intelligible ripple. Meanwhile, the tale of his own voyages, extending over thirty years, suggested to me a *Mardi* in a dozen volumes. He sailed to Takaroa, Amanu, Hikueru and to Rapa, the top of an immense submerged volcano only the crater of which, a splendid harbour, rose about the water. (I supposed this had been the scene of Fenimore Cooper's sea-novel that was called *The Crater*.) At Katiu he was all but drowned in a fearful mill-race near the shore with sharp coral rocks on either side. Of the "dangerous isles," the Tuamotus, he visited sixty or seventy, sometimes staying as long as half a year, listening to legends that seemed to refer to some misty Asiatic homeland and chants and songs that were surely a thousand years old. He found on one island a sage, Te Uira a Maro, the most learned bard of all the Tuamotus who knew more than seven hundred chants, some of which seemed to preserve the memory of a great cataclysm in which the ancient homeland sank into the sea. Frank gathered the ancestral herb-lore of these small coral islands, sometimes inhabited by only two hundred people; then he spent two months on the Mangarevan expedition with Sir Peter Buck, who later became the director of the Bishop Museum. He gathered more legends at Mangareva, a beautiful group, at Pinaki and especially at Vahitahi, the treasure island, for songs and folk-tales, of the whole Pacific, where he obtained a jealously guarded pedigree that carried one back to the gods at the beginning of the world. Sometimes he had been just in time to meet the only surviving bards who knew these old records of the past, for he had arrived in Fagatau shortly before Kamake died, and something similar happened at Vahitahi. He had only a few weeks to see Tuhiragi. The people of the island crowded round his thatched hut at night, singing and telling their stories, and he recorded these roughly on the spot, copying them on his typewriter the following morning. Then he asked the story-tellers to correct his errors.

He was especially eager to recover traces of the old religion, the pagan faith that was banned by the missionaries, while the Mormons, the Catholics and the Protestants alike, believing he meant to revive it,—instead of the mere knowledge of it,— bitterly opposed him. The missionaries tabooed all mention of the god of the underworld, Kiho, together with the phallus-worship of the old Polynesians, on pain, for those who had been baptised, of losing a Christian burial and having no children in the meantime. The cult of Kiho, above all, aroused their ill will when Frank brought forward proofs of its former existence, while others in authority blocked his work because of the erotic element in the old religion. He was haunted by the thought that much of his work might be destroyed, like some of Burton's Arabian collection, on the ground that it was too erotic to be published, and Burton's work might have been replaced while he himself was the only source for these records of the world of the old Polynesians. He had gathered them from sages and chiefs who were no longer living,—some of them went back thousands of years; and he was convinced that if anything happened to these notes of his the Polynesian religion would be lost forever. He had cleared up obscurities and conflicting statements for the whole Pacific about the gods, who appeared now in a consistent light, and he had recovered the lost meanings of esoteric words by finding that the words survived on other islands. For the rest, the magnificent chants and prayers seemed to prove that the Polynesians had not come "up" from savagery but were descended from some great civilization in the Asiatic past; and the erotic was bound up with the noble and the tender. For this reason, Frank refused the offer of a great English press to publish the erotic songs in a splendid edition, unwilling as he was to create the impression that Polynesian literature was erotic to the exclusion of other feelings.

I remember one summer when Frank came home in order to study at Yale again and see Edward Sapir and Roland Dixon, who were to become his ardent supporters at a later day when he also had the approval of Malinowski. After many years he had pieced together what he called the Palae-Polynesian, the root language that was common to the South Sea peoples, Samoans, Hawaiians, Tahitians, Maoris and so on, and, believing that Sanskrit was closely related, he was determined to investigate this,—I think he almost learned it during that summer. As always, he brought with him a battery of fountain pens, black, red and green, for his etymological markings, and the typewriter, built for him, with six kinds of type, rank on rank, and a keyboard like the keyboard of an organ. This *matini pata pata,* as the islanders called it, clattered away in his room from dawn till midnight, when he was not at New Haven, and I could see how it was that, in the land of the beachcomber, Frank in his own way had gone so far. I recalled what Margaret Mead said of the casual South Sea world where no one played for high stakes or paid heavy prices or fought to the death for special ends, so that greatness in art or personality was virtually unknown there. Frank was as much the exception as the "white monk of Timbuctoo" who had also been drawn to the dark peoples, in the African desert,—that other great linguist and scholar who had entered so deeply into the secret places of the native life.

Frank had the intensity and energy of Seabrook's Yacouba and he too, moreover, was a dedicated man. Well he knew the fearful dangers of the weak of will who sank into a beguiling lethargy in the Polynesian world, and he had remarked in one of his letters that the only antidote was "a driving purpose and a burning goal." Fortunately able to toil in heat, he had thriven on a diet of breadfruit and fish, varied with cocoanut and taro, while, as he rode breakers in little boats and often landed on jagged reefs, neither peril, discomfort nor pain ever deterred him. He had gladly put up with the fleas and the lice in the tiny cabins in which he sailed, packed in with pigs and chickens and sacks of coffee, suffering in many ways and threatened with gangrene, to the far eastern Tuamotus and Takapoto. All this misery meant nothing to him if he could find one old island man who had been taught as a child the ancient customs, fortunate as he was himself to be able to work, as he wrote, "with joy at something one loves with wholehearted devotion."

CHAPTER VII

# NEW YORK

ESPECIALLY DURING the *Freeman* years, when we were all on the alert seeking new talents for the paper, I began to take in the vast resources of New York, which was always entertaining angels unawares. It was, at times, the literary capital of half a dozen countries, with poets and prophets in exile from the Ukraine or Siam, Bulgaria, Brazil and Argentina. A few were great writers who lived in the city unrecognized, while trumpery native geniuses triumphed on Broadway,—spokesmen of humanity or national poets who were sometimes under a cloud at home and lived in the deepest obscurity in the Bronx or Brooklyn. This was true in many a case with writers of Latin America whom only Waldo Frank could properly acclaim, victims of revolutions in their own countries. Kahlil Gibran, the Syrian poet, had a large following in New York and his works were published there in a sumptuous edition, for he was well supported by the Syrian merchants; but who was less esteemed or known than the "Goethe of Hungary," as he was called, who lived over an up-town tailor's shop? That, to be sure, was in Hitler's time, when the prodigal city overflowed with many of the great spirits of central Europe. But when did it not abound with similar exiles?

I never lost the feeling of excitement with which I encountered these extraordinary men, whose lives in so many cases were romantic or tragic and whom one sometimes saw at the New School for Social Research in its first little group of red brick buildings. The watchword there was always "Humanity," as distinguished from "Prosperity,"—the rights of man as opposed to the rights of wealth; and there one met Veblen, now wizened and old, with his look of an invalid troll, together with James Harvey Robinson and Charles A. Beard. The age of reason still flourished there and man had not yet "fallen" in the minds of these intelligent humanists who were building the future, or at least felt they were building a future for man who, far from falling, had risen out of slime and protoplasm. They scouted the notion that man was naturally disorderly and had to be held in check by the far-seeing Tory, for it was obvious that men were conservative by nature and all too ready to invent obstacles to change. As against Trotter's herd-mindedness, they preached an ardent faith in what Robinson called "salvation through knowledge and laughter," upholding the "creative" as opposed to the "acquisitive," the note of the business world which they abhorred. It was Bertrand Russell who developed this antithesis, and it may have been at the New School that I first heard the sage who suggested the Mad Hatter of Tenniel's drawing. His voice was like a bagpipe, a low continuous ah-ah-ah out of which, with a louder hum, the words arose.

One voluntary exile, the one whom I myself knew best and with whom I lived for a while at Petitpas', the old artist-philosopher John Butler Yeats, who died in 1922, had also been a child of the age of reason. He scouted the notion that man had fallen and that human nature was essentially bad, an idea he connected with the "dull" Belfast people who were puritans and found it good for business; for he had grown up regarding it as a "gentlemanly trait to think well," as he said, "of our fellow creatures." This was a part of the liberal faith to which I clung instinctively, and so was his belief in the idea of happiness, which he by no means connected with the notion of success. Happiness, from his point of view, was an outward sign of harmony, a concord of all the notes of the man within; but as for the bitch-goddess, whom he had to pretend that he pursued, he naturally cared for this lady nothing at all. Seventy years old when he came to New York, he remained because he saw ahead what he called a "hopeful penury instead of a hopeless." But penury itself had no terrors for him, and he never seemed wiser than when he said,—what Thoreau might have said,—that the "angel of impecuniosity" had not betrayed him. I rode with John Sloan in the first coach at J. B. Yeats's funeral before he was taken away to be buried, under a stone with a Celtic cross, and with W. B. Yeats's inscription, in northern New York state. I almost felt, with Sloan, that I had lost a father; for this "best talker I ever knew," as G. K. Chesterton called him, had been a reassuring presence also in my house. My wife delighted in him, loving the humorous tenderness with which he surveyed our family doings. Once when my older boy ran into a tree and cut his head he recollected how "Willie" as a child had done this, and he said it augured well for my inattentive son, who was plainly also moving in a dream.

What Yeats had been for me, I know that Alfred Stieglitz was for many of my friends, but I never felt at home in the *petite chapelle* either at "291" or the "American Place." It was Stieglitz's line that he who is not with us is against us, somewhat in the manner of Whitman fifty years before, obviously as a result of the feeling, which he shared with the great Walt, that he was involved in a losing battle. Whitman had talked about "our crowd" as if not to be in it meant that you were not merely outside but hostile, and so it was with Stieglitz also. If you could not be his disciple and would not be his enemy, you had to maintain in his presence a certain aloofness. There was, besides, an element of the mystagogue in him, and it irritated people when he pretended that his pictures could not be bought but only "acquired under certain circumstances." This innocent *réclame* was merely a reaction against our shameful cult of advertising, while by holding his light under the bushel he made the light still brighter for those who were under the bushel with him. Stieglitz could have been rich if he had wished to be so, but, scarcely able to maintain his gallery, he said the landlord had supplanted the Lord in the general downfall of art and rejection of the artist. I once heard him say that he would be glad to pile up all his photographs and make a bonfire of them in the middle of the floor, for the world did not deserve to have them in it. But his paranoia made other artists feel that he was one of them, while, standing his ground, he was always there, at all hours of the day or night, like a rock in the sea or a spring in a dry land.

Stieglitz was the sort of man whose life is attended by signs and wonders, coincidences and other notes of the necromancer. Along with the mystagogue, there was an element of the psychic in him, and, once when I was talking with him, thinking, as I talked, "You are, after all, a bit of a Svengali," he said, out loud, pronouncing the word just as I was thinking it, "Someone said the other day that I was a Svengali." But he was more like the Ancient Mariner, with his glittering eye and skinny hand, and the wild tufts of hair that grew out of his ears, who had his will with everyone, for who could choose but hear and listen, when he talked, like a three years' child? The last time I saw him was two weeks before his death. I was walking down Madison Avenue, and, suddenly realizing that I had forgotten just where to find the "American Place," I exclaimed to the listening air, "What *is* Stieglitz's number?" And a voice replied "509." It seemed to come from heaven, but actually it came from a passer-by who had heard me ask the question, apparently one of the millions of ordinary men who roam New York and who walked on with no further remark or interest. Once upstairs, I told Stieglitz about this, but he seemed to take for granted these manifestations. He spoke of a similar occult intervention that had attended his meeting with Frieda Lawrence. Then he said he had been thinking about me because he was reading my son's and my translation of Amiel's Journal, which he was holding in his hand. Stieglitz was seated on a couch, with his disciples about him, like Socrates in the prison in David's picture, as if he too were about to drink the hemlock; and in fact a few days later he was dead. No one could have been serener or sweeter than he was that day; one felt that he had at last spent all his passion.

There were many for whom Stieglitz discovered America in his photographs of the New York streets, of the ferry-boats and the waters surrounding Manhattan, the incoming shiploads of immigrants and the skyline of the city. Meanwhile, the folk-past of the country, so little known heretofore, began to arouse attention in the nineteen-twenties when, at the Whitney Museum, the painter Henry Schnakenberg exhibited his American primitives and related objects. Among these were ship's figureheads and cigar-store Indians, shown for the first time as works of art, an interest in which had begun at Ogunquit with the painters there, Charles Sheeler, Kuniyoshi and certain others. This interest Constance Rourke, whom I saw often during these years, extended to include music, architecture and the work of the Shaker colonies and frontier artists, for she was already investigating a native American aesthetic past that had been scarcely known except in fragments. Constance Rourke, who had taught at Vassar and studied at the Sorbonne, and who wrote often for *The Freeman*, disclosed to me a West of which I had known little, as a reader of *The Ordeal of Mark Twain* could readily see. In part from reading Emerson, I was already prepared to take a more sympathetic view of our old writers and the country, but in certain respects my horizon was indefinitely broadened by Constance Rourke's eager and eloquent studies. She was already preparing for the general history of American culture of which she finished parts before her death; and she wrote, from time to time, to tell me of the proofs she found that America had its own definite aesthetic tradition.

Constance Rourke had been impressed by Herder's theory that, in every country, the fine arts are an outgrowth of the folk arts and that one finds in these the source of a culture. For the texture of the communal experience determined the character of the folk arts, and she was convinced that our culture, derived from Europe, had diverged from Europe in accordance with our own experience and needs. Just as American Calvinism differed from European Calvinism, so all our original patterns of thought and feeling had been "pulled," as she said, "into new dimensional forms"; and, finding that all our derived ideas had been shaped to new distinctive ends, she was bent on creating,—as I was,—a "usable past." (To speak for a moment of the thirties rather than the twenties.) For would not the knowledge and sense of an indigenous tradition nourish the American artists and writers of the future? Obviously, these artists and writers would be more confident and mature if they could feel they were working "in a natural sequence."

Thus, at a time when American writers were deeply concerned with the country and were beginning to explore its spiritual resources, Constance Rourke brought together a thousand concrete evidences of the widespread folk-culture of the national past. She wrote to tell me of some of these, a painting, for instance, in Michigan, "a Matisse-like fruit piece with unusual variations, amazing in transparency of colour and fine design," or the magnificent chimneys and iron doors she had happened upon in ruins of eighteenth-century furnaces and forges. Or she had discovered wall-paintings in New England, quite unknown hitherto, a curious painter whose name was Voltaire Combe, a mass of unknown early music and much, connected with the old frontier, that she brought out in her studies of Audubon and Crockett. I thought of her when I read Waldo Frank's story about the "artist-painter of Illuria, Ohio," for this J. B. Bonabath was the kind of gifted oddity whom she discovered in many a Western town. The personal pleasure in stripped forms and finished plain surfaces that drew her to the Shaker craftsmen as well as to Sheeler,—regarding whom she wrote an elaborate study,—bore witness to her taste for "the good, the life-giving elements in literature," for *bonae literae* as distinguished from *belles lettres*. She regretted that the former phrase should have dropped out of use in favour of the latter, which stressed only beauty, as she regretted the flight from communal expression in the cosmopolitan literature that was coming to the fore.

In this there were many who agreed with her, in the West especially, and it was certainly true that something went out of our literature when the expatriates of the twenties set the new fashion. There was a war henceforth between the writers of the hinterland and those whom they called the "New York critics,"—the urban intelligentsia who stood for the incoming mode,—and whom, for one, Mary Austin resented, like Vachel

Lindsay, who also felt that literature and art are primarily expressions of the people. This was Carl Sandburg's position, too, with all the American counterparts of the Slavophiles of Russia in their struggle with the cosmopolitan worshippers of Western Europe. But for a long time to come the expatriates were to have their way, with tragic results for certain of the hinterlanders not only in writing but in painting. There were the cases of Grant Wood and John Stuart Curry, for instance, both of whom died "broken-hearted,"—or so said their friend Thomas Hart Benton,—convinced as they were that their enemies were right in saying that they had been wholly on the wrong track. So powerful was the new cosmopolitan fashion.

It was in the twenties that I saw most of the rude forefather of us all, then at the height of his influence, Henry L. Mencken, a full-blooded, warm-hearted man who came up from Baltimore every week and joined us now and then at *Freeman* lunches. Nock, especially, delighted in him, but no one could resist him, for he was the personification of a shrewd good nature, or so he always seemed except on one occasion when I saw how unforgiving he could be. It was at a luncheon at the Brevoort that B. W. Huebsch gave in honour of Sherwood Anderson, whom he was publishing, and all the literary world was there, including Stuart P. Sherman, who had attacked Mencken in several essays. But for Sherman much water had gone under the bridge since he had defended "Puritanism" against the modern literary sansculottes,—and had consequently been the darling of the old guard,—and, following Emerson's belief that where there is power there is virtue, he had gone over to the moderns, lock, stock and barrel. The rising star of the reaction had lost his earlier notion that the twentieth century was wholly the work of the devil, and he was already almost at home in the literary circles that he had once regarded

with suspicion and fear. Wishing to bury the hatchet with
Mencken, he asked to be introduced to him and eagerly
crossed the room to shake his hand. But Mencken would have
none of this friendly gesture. He refused even to look at the
eleventh-hour champion with whom he had exchanged blows
not long before.

Thirty years later few remembered Stuart Sherman's extraordinary vogue, and even the real vogue of Mencken was
almost as brief, although it could never have been forgotten
that he was a literary statesman whose strategy and decisions
affected us all. Whether or not one agreed with anything he
wrote, and much as one may have disliked his tone and temper,
he was one of those men who create the climate in which
writers have to live and the currents of thought and feeling that
carry them along. Who could deny that in very large measure
his essay *The Sahara of the Bozart* was the first cause of the
rebirth of writing in the South?—and Mencken opened the
public mind to the writing of the new racial groups in a literature that was exclusively Anglo-Saxon. With him came in the
realism that had been almost smothered under the evasive ideal-
ism of the recent past, and all these were major acts in what
this German-American called the new Aufklärung in the republic. He had cleared away the provincialism in our literary
atmosphere, he had "defaced the coinage" in the manner of
Diogenes, obliterating the mint-marks of false conventions.
Who, moreover, aroused more interest in the American scene
than this new humorous Gulliver in his home-bound travels
who saw his fellow-countrymen as Brobdingnagians and
Houyhnhnms, monstrous, to be laughed at certainly, but never
ignored?

It was a pity, for the rest, that, with his great influence, he
should have known nothing of the past of the country, to

which he was even hostile by temperament and training; and it was also unfortunate that he stopped dead as a critic at the age when the critical mind begins to mature. As for Mencken's "American language," as a literary medium I could not believe in this at all, for it seemed to me that serious writers would always be far more concerned to explore the wonderful resources of traditional English. Where did one find the American language in Mencken's own books, I mean in his own best expository writing, and where did one find it in Willa Cather or Katherine Anne Porter or Thornton Wilder or Edmund Wilson or even Hemingway or Faulkner? It was a pity, finally, that Mencken should have become the dupe of his own stage-personality as a Hitlerite or Hun, an extreme case of the tough-guy pose of those who, for nothing in the world, would ever be taken, in American eyes, for sissies. Having assumed a persona or mask that was at variance with his real self, he felt he had to be consistent with it, and he became a Hitlerite out of bravado. The man who wrote the essay *The Poetry of Christianity,* undoubtedly an expression of his real feelings, had nothing in common with the man who said the ignorant should be encouraged to spawn in order to keep up a steady supply of slaves.

There was no touch of the American language in the tales of Scott Fitzgerald, the typical writer of the twenties, as he seemed later, whom I saw now and then with the friend of my childhood Maxwell Perkins, the publisher who regarded him almost as a son. Scott Fitzgerald wrote to me in praise of my book on Henry James and he said he knew *The Ordeal of Mark Twain* also; then he sent me a copy of *The Great Gatsby* from Capri, where he was staying in 1925. He had found in a bookshop there *America's Coming-of-Age,* which he had bought and read "with enormous pleasure,"—the book that

Huneker reviewed and Carl van Doren read, standing, beside a shelf of new accessions. It was "virtually the first book to voice the new age," Carl van Doren wrote to me at a time when I was scarcely aware that anyone had read it.

I remember a dinner at Ernest Boyd's at which Scott Fitzgerald and Zelda, his wife, arriving an hour late when the others had finished, sitting at table fell asleep over the soup that was brought in, for they had spent the two previous nights at parties. So Scott Fitzgerald said as he awoke for a moment, while someone gathered Zelda up, with her bright cropped hair and diaphanous gown, and dropped her on a bed in a room near by. There she lay curled and asleep like a silky kitten. Scott slumbered in the living-room, waking up suddenly again to telephone an order for two cases of champagne, together with a fleet of taxis to take us to a night-club. That moment and scene bring back now a curious note of the twenties that one did not connect with insanity or tragedy then, while I was drawn to the Scott Fitzgeralds, whom I never really knew but who seemed to me, so obviously, romantic lovers.

CHAPTER VIII

# WESTPORT

Mᴏʀᴇ ᴀɴᴅ more, as the twenties advanced, the "exurban-ites" settled in Westport,—those displaced New York-ers, brightly so called, who lived beyond the suburbs but who remained urbanites at heart. As the inventor of the phrase ob-served, they "set the styles and moulded the fashions and peo-pled the dreams of the country," for they were artists, writers and fashion-designers. A few were young men who had sat on terraces outside the Dôme and the Rotonde; and presently, when the summer theatre was well established, I saw Piran-dello on the main street one day. He was peering into a peram-bulator and playing with a baby's toes, no doubt on his way to a rehearsal. But whom and what did one not see in this little town that stood for the resurgence of the moment in the life of the country? A dealer soon opened a gallery there with a show of Rouault and another of Canaletto, Tiepolo and Guardi. Then Cardinal Pacelli, later the Pope, appeared in a Westport garden at a play on a biblical theme that was written by a neighbour. Said he to the author, "There should be more plays like that."

Westport, with the towns roundabout, was the "archetype of exurbs . . . the richest in exurban manifestations,"—to quote the ingenious Spectorsky once again,—one of which was "Cactus" Moore, who was often seen fishing from the bridge when he

was not sitting for a cartoon in *The New Yorker*. It was supposed that this cowboy from Texas concocted half the new
smart words, together with the topical phrases that spread
through the country, passed on by him to the illustrators whom
he served as a model and popularized soon after on the stage in
New York. Then there was Rose O'Neill, who lived in a
pseudo-Italian villa, a fairy-tale house with a fairy-tale name,
in a clearing in the woods beside the river, overlooking a
sunken garden with a pool surrounded by her handiwork,
drooping nude sculptured figures of uncertain sex. In her flowing pink draperies, Rose O'Neill, with bright blonde hair about
her neck, embraced a crowd of followers who lived on her
bounty, for this creator of the Kewpie doll could not quickly
enough divest herself of the fortune that she had made from it.
She endowed at the Hotel Brevoort a circular table, and there
anyone who called himself a poet or a painter could charge to
her account whatever he wished. She herself and the famous
doll figured in the frescoes that John Stuart Curry painted in
the hall of the high school,—for Curry also lived in a grove
by the river,—and in these frescoes he painted as well Theodore
Dreiser and Eugene O'Neill with Sherwood Anderson and
James Earle Fraser, the sculptor. Of me he made a red-chalk
portrait drawing that gave me the look of a Mexican border
bandit. I asked him, whilst he was working on this, what
type in his boyhood in Kansas the boys he had known had
most admired,—was it the big bear hunter or the millionaire
farmer? No, said Curry, the minister was the hero of the boys.
The minister was the type they all looked up to, as they had
looked up to the pilot in Mark Twain's Missouri.

Once Rose O'Neill appeared in our garden, in her pink
satin with the golden slippers in which she had walked two
miles from Carabas. It was a May afternoon and the leaves had

just unfolded,—one had almost heard them unfolding in the last week of April, when the squirrel with the bitten ear frisked in the great oak over the roof and everything growing or flying seemed aquiver with excitement. The tulips and the hyacinths blossomed on the rocky slope, and one caught the secret flight of the robin darting from its nest with wings close to the body so as not to be noticed. The bittersweet vine that Mrs. La Farge had sent us from Saunderstown spread new shoots over the lattice by the door of the study, and tendrils with clusters of lettuce-green leaves straggled out from the dark green patch that covered most of the slope with English ivy. This had all grown from a slip that was brought by an artist who had owned our house from Sir Walter Scott's Abbotsford in Scotland. It occurred to me that cuttings from this might please someone in the South, so I sent a boxful to Miss Mary Johnston, the old Virginia novelist who had written *To Have and to Hold* and *Prisoners of Hope*. She planted the ivy outside her study windows beside our friend Edward Sheldon's rose-tree, and she said it brought her visions of Melrose and Thomas the Rhymer, while she heard the pibroch about the house at night.

For a good part of a year we had Henry Stuart living with us,—Henry Longan Stuart, who reviewed for the *Times* and who wrote the fine novel *Weeping Cross*,—a romantic Englishman of Irish descent and a Catholic of an old English type like some of the cavaliers who fought in the Low Countries. He might have been, in fact, one of the Templars of the first crusades, for, well-born, poor and exempt from worldly ties, he really had all the traits that characterized them. Henry turned his Irish wit against the "Celtic twilight" from which "at any moment a brickbat might emerge," for he was much concerned about the treachery that had caused such havoc in the history of the Irish. A captain in the British army in Italy, he had been wounded and thrown from his horse, then, remaining in Florence for several years, he had lived on a Colorado ranch before he came East as a literary soldier of fortune. Translating many Italian books, he wrote poems in a seventeenth-century mode that could only be found later in old magazines,—for the typewritten book of his poetry was lost after his death,—while *Weeping Cross* recalled the seventeenth century too, alike in tone, style, setting, characters and story. It related the adventures of a cavalier much like himself in the New England of Hawthorne's *The Scarlet Letter,* a soldier half gallant, half monk, and his desperate love affair with a volatile and still more beautiful Hester Prynne. The more or less archaic style, so often a cumbersome device, admirably completed here the illusion of the story.

Extremely attractive to women, Henry was equally drawn to them, while he recoiled from the sexual promiscuity that was so general after the first world war. I remember how he once repulsed a proposal over the telephone. "Madam," his answer was, "you should apply to your husband in matters of that kind." To this the lady replied, "What, you say that! You with a face like yours!" But Henry's face had tragic memories in it, and he knew why the Stoics so carefully controlled their sexual life if only in the interest of their peace of mind. It was a question with him of all or nothing, and he vaguely planned a book in praise of chastity that would have been unique in the twenties I remember. For chastity had come to be defined as merely a convention based on fear that had lost all meaning in a day of contraceptives. Henry remembered William James's characterization of chastity as the principle of all human social elevation,—the subjecting of every present incitement of sense to suggestions of aesthetic or moral fitness;

and he agreed with Albert Nock about the barbaric regression which the "sex" novels of the moment represented. In many of these novels the relations of the sexes were physical merely and therefore undiversified and exactly alike, and what could art do with this characterless subject-matter, sensationally exciting as perhaps it might be? Nock, in his *Memoirs*, wondered why novelists no longer attempted to show how interesting the relations of the sexes could be when they had no physical element in them, as, for example, in the well-known case of d'Alembert and Mlle. de Lespinasse. Henry himself was involved in relations of this kind, and these were almost as complex as the relations between Freud and his wife in the story of this great man's courtship and marriage. Ironical it seemed to me, when I read Ernest Jones's biography, that Freud should have been the father of so many "sex" novels, for this monogamist's own love story contained all the elements which these novels of our time wholly omitted. "With him the word 'puritanical' would not be out of place," Ernest Jones remarked in this connection; and everything in his story was "character," nothing was "sex."

At Westport Henry fell in again with his old friend Hugh Lofting, for he had known well as a boy in England this somewhat dandified lover of snuff who was writing there the "Dr. Dolittle" stories. Hugh Lofting had a study in the woods not far from our house. Then Henry knew Brooks Atkinson, the theatre critic of the *New York Times*, a paradox, a naturalist whose model was Thoreau and who lived in a state of tension between two vocations. No doubt this invigorated both. At least, I know that his country essays were among the liveliest of their kind and time, delightful to one who scarcely followed his theatrical reviews because, in the country, I could not follow the theatre. In Westport I never missed a chance to see him. Once he came out to find again a Wilson's thrush that lived in a shadowy glen on the road to Redding. As we were driving there, he described the tree where the bird should be found; and, sure enough, there he was, almost on the expected branch, as if he were keeping a rendezvous with this great bird-lover. It seemed to me a case of ornithological second sight, worthy of the bird's namesake, Alexander Wilson.

One creator of the New York stage who often came to visit us was my old Harvard friend Lee Simonson, the stage-designer of the Theatre Guild whose first wish had been to paint, in Paris, in the circle of the Steins, Leo and Gertrude. Lee was ill at ease with what he called the anæmia of the American eye, the sallowness and greyness of the typical American palette, tints of oatmeal and sand, as he described them; and he had once noticed, approaching Naples, that the Americans on board the ship had marvelled at the prospect through smoked glasses. With his marked Oriental air,—he said that in a mosque once he was asked why he did not speak Arabic,—Lee had a special taste for brilliant colours, for startling tints in shirts and ties that were usually kept for the Negro trade, as a dealer told him on one occasion. Lee had been drawn to Gauguin because he restored these pure colours that were so alien to the coldness and dullness of New York, and, enchanted in Paris with Cézanne and Picasso, he was especially taken with Matisse's violent colour oppositions. He felt it was his mission to introduce this colour into the neutral background of contemporary living; but, hoping at first to do mural decoration, he soon became convinced that he had set out to learn his craft too late. For his critical faculty was so over-developed that he felt, when he was painting, tormented and strained. Then, seeing his first modern décor in the Ballet Russe of Diaghilev, he realized that the Art Theatre was his true sphere, and he had come home to find playwrights, producers and actors who were bent on revolutionizing the stage in New York.

Lee's personal hero was Bernard Shaw, for whom he did some of his best work, while we all belonged to the generation whose earliest recollection of the stage had been Joseph Jefferson in *Rip van Winkle*. Lee, in our Westport house,—a manic-depressive,—was usually aglow, counselling my wife on the raising of lilies or my boys on the making of beer or planting his choicest dahlia bulbs in the garden. Once, I remember, when we had imprudently rented the house, these bulbs, stored in the cellar, vanished in our absence, and, as they looked exactly like sweet potatoes, we supposed our tenants must have eaten them. Lee had long telephone conversations with Alfred Lunt in the far West,—I think about *Amphitryon 38,*—and, if it rained, he would telephone his children to be sure to wear their proper coats and rubbers. For he was a most meticulous model parent. Meanwhile, between plays, he wrote the essays that appeared in *Minor Prophecies* or in later issues of *The New Republic,* essays in which he shunned the note of the typical critique of the time,—"usually a dress rehearsal for the Last Judgment." He said to me once, "The other fellow's grass is always greener," meaning that writing always seemed more attractive when he was deep in theatre work, but he found writing painful and reading his proofs, he remarked, was like walking in leaden shoes through hot wet sand. Lee, sometimes regarded as blustering and rude, was certainly not modest,—when he was in high spirits he seemed to me like a brass band playing in the house,—but he was the most winning and generous of men and, far from being vain, he had the profound humility of the true-blue artist. With this went, moreover, a copious flow of ideas and the learning that later marked *The Stage is Set*.

Lee said his ideas were corks in a current; but I believe that in *Minor Prophecies* he was the first to suggest a number that were developed presently by others. He had applied to the American museum some of the notions of design that he had worked out also on the stage, recommending early the arranging of objects in period rooms or grouping them to show their relation to the whole structure of their epoch. The rooms in the old museums had been so crammed with objects that the mere process of attention was an agony of effort, and crowding five great works into a space where not one could truly live seemed to him as criminal as the crowding of tenement bedrooms. This accumulation displayed everything and revealed nothing, and Lee as a painter had been depressed by these vast dreary asylums where shelter was accorded to the waifs and strays of art. He was all for a new museum in which apses were built into walls, perhaps with altars under stained-glass windows, and with reliquaries, bishops' crooks, tapestries and lamps. Then Lee suggested the renting of new pictures for brief periods at a low price, a sort of "trial marriage" between the renter and the picture that might well result in an ultimate purchase, a notion that seemed suited to an experimental time, an age of small apartments and constant moving. Lee himself liked to try things out. He designed ballets for Mordkin; and he once bought and produced a play, well knowing, as he wrote to me, that "only masochists become theatrical producers and only sadists congratulate them."

When I thought ill of Santayana, I had to remember how many of my friends owed everything to his *Reason in Art* and *The Sense of Beauty*. "Let us live in the mind," Santayana's saying, had made a deep impression on the sensitive Lee, and "If it weren't for him," Lee said to me later, "I shouldn't be engaged on my present opus." He was referring to *The Stage is Set,* the great study of stage-design to which he returned whenever engagements were lagging and in which he spoke for the community theatres that played so large a part in our friend Lewis Mumford's regional planning. For scenic design, from Lee's point of view, was an interpretative art that served the needs of society, social and moral, and he believed that all artists should be socially minded and must make their work necessary to society if they were to survive. So he was to write in *Part of a Lifetime,* and he might have been thinking of the great Mexican painters who were so deeply involved in the revolution in their country. "We are all preachers," Lee said to me once; and he said again, "We are all prophets, Puritans like you and Hebrews like Waldo and myself. But," he added, "the practice of letters is a cause, and it will have to be kept one. Or made one again."

What he had in mind here was my notion of the artist and writer as a leader or pathfinder,—a sort of guru,—or what Paul Rosenfeld meant when he spoke of the poet as "the man who can give the race the direction in which it has to go." All our generation had some such belief as this, and nothing marked it off more clearly from the age that followed, the age of John Crowe Ransom and the "new" critics. Literature, for these men, had no public function; they had entirely relinquished, as Ransom said, the notion of the poet as a prophet or a priest; whereas the great writers who had formed our minds had felt it was part of their task "to improve the prevailing order of the world."

I am quoting Ibsen, who also said that literature should be not only "revelative" but "redemptive," a notion that was soon to vanish from the literary mind and that came to seem contemptible and even absurd. But, certain as I felt myself that it was unassailable and destined sooner or later to rearise, I re-

membered through all the coming time the great men who had
stood for it, Ruskin, Emerson, Tolstoy, Romain Rolland; and,
running through earlier centuries, how many could one count?
One and all would have agreed with Chekhov that the "good"
writers convey "a sense of what life ought to be" and that
they are "summoning you towards it," while they have "an
object, immediate or remote, the abolition of serfdom, the happiness of humanity and so on." Had not Strindberg observed
of the artist that he was a "lay preacher," a name in which
Anthony Trollope and Mark Twain rejoiced, as Bernard Shaw
said that the "man of letters, when he is more than a mere
confectioner, is a prophet or nothing." Even Kipling said he
had a "mission to preach." As it seemed to me, the sole condition was that one should not professedly preach or make direct
appeals to the conscious will, and I was not greatly disturbed
when I was called a preacher. I remembered that Isadora Dun-
can had been convinced that her dancing might, as a new form
of religion, regenerate the world, while I was aware of the comic
aspects of the "uplift" tendencies of our national life that were
also, in their reformism, connected with preaching. Convinced as I was that writing was truly a vocation, I was convinced also that literature and art existed for the sake of what
Berenson called "life-enhancement,"—making this planet "fit
for human habitation,"—as I shared Walt Whitman's belief
that "first-class works are to be tried by their eligibility to free,
arouse, dilate." I sympathized with Whitman's praise of the
novelists Cooper and Scott because, as he said, they "take life
forward," believing that this would always stand for the major strain in literature, however one admired the various minor
strains.

Some years later, Ford Madox Ford, in *This Was the Nightingale*, expressed the opposing views of these two generations.

"The business of art," he said, "is not to elevate but to render," adding, "Those are the two schools of thought that have eternally divided humanity, and no one in the end will ever know which will win out." *To render* was the aim of the coming generation, just as *to elevate* was the aim of ours; and I never doubted that our "school" would come into its own again when writers tired of "rendering" as their ultimate object. How limited their notion was of literature and art as a game or a "superior amusement"! Our school stood for the old humanist dream of "building a garden in the cosmic wilderness,"—to quote the grandfather of the Huxleys of our time; and it was obvious that humankind could not dispense forever with writers who were devoted to a cause like that. Lee shared my point of view, sceptical as he sometimes was regarding the general influence of great writers, saying, for instance, in a letter to me, "Each age goes about its business like freighters in a harbour. A little of the force that drives it leaks out as a surplus, like oil on harbour waters. For a moment it is iridescent, and beautiful in the right light. But the business of shipping the cargoes of any epoch goes its own way." He wrote again, "I dislike admitting it but I have begun to despair about the relation of literature to life. What are its central images and ideas but occasional solace and occasionally a pastime to the vast majority who live to possess—women, gold, power, political or industrial? It seems to me we make the mistake of persons employed at a mint who like the bas-reliefs stamped on a surface so much that they end by imagining the coins are made for coin collectors. Perhaps they are, ultimately, but they are spent by people to whom it makes no difference whether they are handling the *livre tournois,* or, when that becomes obsolete, the *louis d'or,* or, when that has to be hoarded,—a remnant of another golden age,—get on just as well with handsomely engraved pieces of paper." But, having said this, Lee wrote again, "Though I can admit this in general, I can't as yet admit it in regard to the particular field in which I am a tenant. I end my book [*The Stage is Set*] with a noble howl to the philosopher-poets to arise and save the theatre. And now that it is written I'm quite certain that they won't."

So much for what Lee somewhere called the "irrepressible evangelism" that marked the American character,—and touched our own,—a trait we still shared in a way with the novelists of the muckraking time and the surviving college-settlement writers. Among these were the novelist Robert Herrick, Edgar Lee Masters and Vachel Lindsay, all of whom had lived at Hull House in Chicago, where our friend Francis Hackett had found what he called an "American faith" in place of the usual patter of success and smartness. All these men felt they were somehow involved in the great human adventure that James Harvey Robinson described in his books, pursuing the good of humanity as their chief interest in the face of tribal society and its sanctified blindness. Our Westport neighbour Lillian Wald symbolized this pursuit, along with certain women I met at her house, among them Grace Abbott of the Children's Bureau, Alice Hamilton, the Harvard professor, and Jane Addams, who spent summers on the Connecticut river. I remember Jane Addams's remark that the river was "so friendly," with the oil-barges drifting up and down. These "exemplary women," in the old phrase, resembled the devoted souls who tried so soon to establish the Spanish republic,—"do-gooders," one and all, the wisecrack of the smaller souls who wished to pull them down to their own level. For how many strangers, with her courage and glow, had not Lillian Wald, at the port of New York, vindicated America as the land of promise?— while, with her copious peacefulness, her deep simplicity and her repose, Jane Addams suggested Demeter, the earth-mother. A few persons whom I have met have instantly called up for me images of the ancient goddesses and gods,—for one, Alexander Calder in his Hephæstic workshop, my neighbour, the iron-worker deity of the mobiles. Then there was Boardman Robinson, the shapely painter. "Mike" Robinson, naked on a beach, turning hand-springs on the sand, might have given birth to the myth of Bacchus, and I thought of Paul Robeson, years ago, as a kind of Negro Jupiter, thanks to his incomparably spacious voice and presence. Jane Addams had this air of indubitable greatness.

Once, at Lillian Wald's house, I took part in a conversation between Jane Addams and Charles Beard, whom we often went to see in his big slate-coloured house overlooking the Housatonic valley at New Milford. Jane Addams asked him why he had resigned from Columbia and why John Dewey had not done so,—to recall an academic incident of the previous decade,—and the question arose whether Dewey's acceptance of the status quo there was not the logical result of his pragmatism. Dewey's integrity was never in doubt, and Jane Addams, for the rest, defended pragmatism with a shake of her head, saying, "I have seen so many people who thought they were right,"—for every crank in Chicago had haunted Hull House. She turned the subject off, as wise old people are apt to do, partly because they have heard too many discussions, but it struck me as odd that she should remember the people who thought they were right and were not, forgetting those who thought they were right and were so. I remembered her old adoration of Tolstoy, for instance. While the feeling of moral certitude had surely caused much of the evil of the world, had it not initiated more that was good? Charles Beard had not pragmatized when he destroyed his own teaching career by standing up for two colleagues with whom he disagreed, glad to accept, in his contempt for inquisitions and alien control, the insults of certain vulgarians among the trustees. He told me that one of them said to him, "Why do you resign? Don't you know that it's easier for us to find a good professor than a good butler?"

Charles Beard, at his dairy-farm on the ridge over the Housatonic,—in his immense straw hat, haying with his men,—had, more than anyone else I knew, except perhaps Albert Nock, the air and port of one of the founding fathers. He brought back the atmosphere of the early republic, when men were creating a nation and knew they could do so, one of the great pamphleteers of 1776,—he put me in mind of Thomas Paine. He had the same eye for humbugs and shams and the faith in perfectibility, together with a hearty bonhomie and simplicity of nature, and, occasionally wrong-headed as he certainly was, and limited on the poetic side, he was an irreplaceable antiseptic. How valuable was his exposure of the "historical necromancers," along with the assumptions of historical "science."

At New Canaan, closer by, our old friend Maxwell Perkins lived, and Padraic and Mollie Colum spent a number of years in the town, in their accustomed setting of poetry and poets. For one, they knew Bliss Carman, who had taken up quarters at an inn where I spent a winter in New Canaan and who, with his long cloak and his picturesque hair, personified the romantic poet that no one in the new time wished to be. But nothing could have suggested less the glamour of a poet's life than the poor bare little room in which he existed, with nothing visible in it but a bed and a chair, and it was good to know that in his native Canada he was by no means without honour. For who spoke of this poet any longer in New York? He recalled to me the atrocious indifference of our literary world, which tossed away yesterday's talents when they were still active, a fate one could never have foreseen at the time for Edna Millay's rival, the only other reigning woman poet. Elinor Wylie was also living in New Canaan, and there, and at our Westport house, I met this author of *Black Armour*, a phrase that evoked for me an image of herself; for there was something metallic about her and, if not reptilian, glittering and hard, as of some creature living in an iridescent shell. She entered a room with clanking scales, full panoplied for war, like Bonduca or an elegantly slim Valkyrie. This poet was armed at all points, unlike Vachel Lindsay, at the height of his career, the inventor of a new kind of poetry, related to ragtime, who was all too easily made a fool of. Gamaliel Bradford told me later how, in his Wellesley drawing-room, the college girls egged Vachel Lindsay on, baiting this hobbledehoy of genius who was driven at last to suicide, aware of the self-conscious awkwardness of his theatrical declaiming. But I was transported at the Colums' house by the beauty of *The Chinese Nightingale* when, as if in a trance, he recited this poem, repeating the lines that were magical to me, swaying back and forth before the fire.

It was in the twenties that I first met Thomas Wolfe, then still unknown, I think, at the house of Max Perkins,—the giant from the Southern hills, with his puzzled earnest air, who was so soon to begin a momentous career. He was almost as bitter about Jefferson Davis as Sherwood Anderson had been, at Westport,—with far less reason,—about Robert E. Lee, in revolt as he was, and as one saw in *The Hills Beyond*, against the unreality of the legend of the old South. Scarcely knowing who Wolfe was, I was astonished by the animus with which he attacked the new Southern agrarian movement, the

school of the "Fugitive" poets and critics who were bent on
reviving, as he feared, the old regime and all that was fraudu-
lent in it. They pretended that the old regime had favoured
art and literature, dreaming of an aristocratic South that, as
everybody knew, had actually despised the artist and the writer.
Thomas Wolfe recalled to me the diatribes of Mark Twain,
who expressed for these delusions a similar contempt.

I was only then becoming aware of the new movement in
criticism that was emerging in the South with the "formalist"
critics, paralleling the movement in Russia in the opening
years of the first world war whose motto was "Art is always
independent of life." These Russians had cared for form alone,
saying, in the words of one of them, that literature was "a
phenomenon solely of language" and that Gogol's heroes
merely happened to be Russian officials and squires, a fact that
had no more importance than their surroundings. But, whereas
the formalist school in Russia disappeared within two or three
years, the American school was to flourish for decades to come,
devoted to "structural analysis," to the study of "balance and
shifts of tone" and to "functional ambiguities of reference and
syntax." (I am quoting certain of its phrases.) It was almost
to realize Anatole France's prophecy in *La Vie Littéraire* that
"criticism, the youngest of all the literary forms," would "perhaps end by absorbing all the others." As I observed what
seemed to me the blight these "close" critics spread abroad, I
felt they envisaged a literature

> No belly and no bowels,
> Only consonants and vowels,

in the phrase, oddly enough, of John Crowe Ransom. Could
any influence be more sterilizing? And would not this analyti-
cal thinking destroy in readers, in the end, their power of

fantasy and their poetic feeling? I thought of Darwin who said he became conditioned by science to such a degree that he could no longer read a novel. It was Joel Spingarn who first used the phrase "the new criticism," and how would he have felt about grammarians of this kind with their categorical tone and esoteric language? As for me, these "young men rushing into criticism,"—in Ransom's phrase,—caused me to withdraw, slowly, in the other direction; for I scarcely wished any longer to be called a critic when the word assumed these connotations.

## CHAPTER IX

# A HUMANIST

I THINK IT was in 1922 that my friend Hendrik van Loon became, for a number of years, a Westport neighbour,—"the last of the old-fashioned liberals" whom the Smithsonian wanted to buy, as he said once, for its collection. This so-called prince of popularizers was treated with contempt by certain professional historians and many critics, and in fact his personality was more significant than his work, for he usually wrote without tension, *en pantoufles*. But Hendrik was in no sense a literary hack. Hasty as he may have been, his writings were all of a piece, consistent unfoldings of his own special nature, so that he was unique as one of the characters of his time as well as a public figure of importance. Among what George Orwell called the "smelly little orthodoxies" that were already winning so many minds, he was regarded often as a formidable person, and Maxim Gorky said that Hendrik was one of two historians who could be regarded as dangerous to Soviet Russia. Gorky's other historian was Oswald Spengler. For Hendrik fought every kind of tyranny over the mind of man, and, once aroused, he fought with great effect. Moreover, he returned the contempt of the specialists and pedants. Hendrik lived in the large air of the *homo universalis*, a true belated man of the Renaissance, a Dutchman who recalled his beloved Erasmus and who had his own wide learning and zest for life.

He was already an institution and soon became still more so as the author of *Van Loon's Geography* and *Van Loon's Lives,*—in which he appeared as a rather too talkative Plutarch,—the kind of showman who was least respected in an age of cerebration and who seemed to lounge in his books, too much at his ease. Even his plenitude was regarded with suspicion, for Hemingway's "Not too damned much" was a motto of the time. But of Hendrik one could say that, unlike ordinary popularizers, he was inside whatever he wrote about, whether music, his first passion, or the painting in which he might have excelled, or cooking, navigation, ships or maps. From his early childhood these matters were all in his blood. In the Dutch stone cottage he built at Westport, frescoing the walls himself,—he had been asked to do murals for the Waldorf-Astoria in New York,—the study was also a music room, for he had learned to fiddle at ten when he had played Mozart and Haydn with his music-master. Crossing the ocean later, he made friends with Einstein, and the two played in the ship's orchestra together, as Hendrik had played at Munich, with the Schrammelspieler, in his student days, musical orgies that lasted till all hours of the morning. He might have been one of the Dutchmen of old who carried their lutes to the tavern, amusing the tosspots all night with their songs, producing at the same time a copy of Horace and translating some of the odes into a semblance of Dutch.

In the Westport study, his writing-table was littered, like the chairs, with sketches, old maps, atlases, manuals of cooking, and with books in six or seven tongues, one of them Russian, which he had learned in St. Petersburg as a young man. Old atlases had been a part of the household furniture when he was a boy, "both theatre and movie to me in Rotterdam," he said, with maps of the golden age of the Dutch explorers and navigators when some of the cartographers were admirable artists. To them he owed largely his feeling for history and the adventure connected with it, which the modern specialized historians had ceased to feel, and he found that old maps were more apt to give him ideas than pictures or even letters of the past. As a boy in a Dutch port, he had learned to spell, moreover, in the advertisements of ships that were sailing for the Indies. For the rest, he delighted in culinary books, with recipes of the seventeenth century, when Richelieu invented mayonnaise, a characteristic taste of his that figured in the drawings, imaginative, witty and gay, which appeared in his books.

Sketching often with coloured inks, Hendrik captured in a few lines all manner of historic atmospheres, persons and places, Rome in the eighteenth century, Mohammed's Medina or his favourite Thomas Jefferson at Monticello. As in this case, he liked to picture a land overflowing with honey and a table with savoury fowls and bottles of wine, bright bouquets of flowers and bowls of fruit, symbols of liberality and abundance; and he was especially drawn to Jefferson because this great man had won his wife with the violin that he always carried with him. It even went far with Hendrik that Frederick the Great played the flute; and, regarding Emerson, his only complaint was that this humanist had been brought up in the doctrine that you must not notice what you eat. Hendrik liked to think of the times when music and all the other arts were interwoven with the general business of living, from which they were never separated in feeling or thought, and for this he almost condoned the Middle Ages that had, for him, so little common sense. He liked to remember that emperors considered it an honour to be associated with the minnesingers, especially as the troubadour, the minstrel, had been his first ideal of the good life. Hendrik felt that he belonged to a race whose roots were deeply struck into the Rabelaisian earth of the mediæval time, as one saw in the simple folk of both Zealand and Flanders, and he was at home in the whimsicalities, the drolleries, jocosities, quiddities and quips that pleased people four hundred years ago. It struck me that, somehow, his unpretentious drawings recalled the illuminations of the old Netherlandish monks.

Two themes that recurred in these drawings were the Dutch galleon in full sail and the steeple-hatted Dutchman in leather breeches, who appeared as the type figure in many of them, indicating, as it seemed to me, that his imagination was deeply involved in the great age of Holland. It was noticeable that when he was pleased, or otherwise moved or distracted, he always fell back into his native tongue, or at least uttered a few words of it; and nothing could have been more Dutch than his appearance and mode of life in what might have passed for a courtlier Frans Hals's household. (Especially when the baby-chair that had been Emerson's chair as a child was occupied by one of Hendrik's grandsons; for Hendrik had married a great-granddaughter of the "practical navigator" Bowditch and this chair was a gift of the Emersons to a family friend. Well I remember the little red walnut cane-bottomed chair that was fitted for a child of eighteen months.) Hendrik said rightly that if he were dressed in black velvet and frills he would have looked like one of Van der Helst's portraits, gigantic as in fact he was, so that not only his suits and his shirts but also his boots and his hats were made for him. (Until he gave up hats and went about in snowstorms wrapped in his huge ulster but bare-headed.) He said that in berths in sleeping-cars he had to fold up like a jack-knife; and once when, later, he came for a visit after he had left Westport, we were obliged to rebuild a bed for him. The sides had to be extended about four inches. Coming back from Finland once, he told me how Sibelius had met him with the words, "Willkommen! Willkommen! How good it is to see another man who can fold his arms round his belly and laugh!"

Sibelius, who had read him and asked him for a visit, agreed that only laughter could save the world, a notion suggesting not only Frans Hals but many another Hollander of the days when Holland was the centre of the civilized world. Hendrik dwelt lovingly on those six decades when the "pancake of mud" on the North Sea ruled millions of people, red, yellow and black, when it supplied all Europe with grain, fish, whale-bones, linen and hides and its storehouses burst with bales of nutmeg and pepper. Then Descartes lived in Amsterdam and thither all roads led that were travelled by artists and writers, scientists and statesmen, and learned geographers made the charts by which all the world sailed, with atlases printed on presses named after the muses. Then lived Van Dieman of Van Dieman's Land and Tasman of Tasmania, and from Spitz-bergen to Staten Island, New Zealand and Mauritius, the Dutch were pioneers of navigation. Formerly the music-masters of all the other races, they had become supremely a nation of painters, and every Dutch village had its painter as, later, every New England village had its mechanical genius and inventor of gadgets. Then Holland, the greatest of international count-ing-houses, harboured Spinoza, Grotius, Vondel and Rem-brandt.

Half a dozen of Hendrik's books grew out of his pride in these great days when one small country could not hold the people who were driven wild with excitement by the sight of maps, when the Dutch ports were crowded with ships that bulged with whale-oil, spices, silks, and the streets suggested a continual county fair. There were splendid paintings on every hand, and Swedes, Turks, Blackamoors, East Indians, Germans and Frenchmen brought the whole world to every Dutchman's door, a memory that made Hendrik feel as if he had been born with the twentieth-century planetary outlook. As a child in Rotterdam he had spent days in the Museum of the Knowledge of This Earth where he first made acquaintance with the world and its wonders and where the figure of a Laplander hitching a reindeer to a sleigh gave him his first longing to explore it. Other days he spent on an old training-vessel, for he had an uncle in the Dutch navy, and there was nothing he did not know about the rigging of the ships that were to appear in so many of his drawings. He read books on polar exploration,—Nansen was his hero,—and especially on the Dutch explorers who aroused his interest in geography and history and the age in which they themselves were paramount. Learning English in *Henry Esmond,* he had found Motley as captivating as American boys found *Huckleberry Finn,* and he evoked the Dutch republic in his *Peter Stuyvesant* and in his book about Rembrandt, *R.v.R.* His wish here was to excavate seventeenth-century Holland as Schliemann had excavated the city of Troy, and this was the one book he hoped to be remembered for, a book that, with all its *longueurs,* may well survive. Hendrik's chief reward, I think, was that it won for him a letter of high praise from Willa Cather.

The book was a sort of *Kulturroman,* like *The Cloister and the Hearth,* in which appeared Hendrik's idol Erasmus, the winning humanist and scholar whom he sketched as often as he sketched musical instruments, fruit and ships. At the age of five, on his way to school, in the care of the old family servant Hein, he had passed every day the birthplace and statue of Erasmus, whom he had followed a few years later by going to school at Gouda, where he too had learned his Greek and Latin. This reasonable, witty, tolerant man was Hendrik's lifelong model in all respects, good manners, temper, learning, the first "guest" in *Van Loon's Lives,* in which he was constantly present, an affinity of the author of the book. Hendrik liked to recall that Erasmus was also an amateur musician, and he poured out his affection for him in the long introduction he wrote in time for Erasmus's *In Praise of Folly.* In this book he found a world in which man was free from the violence, prejudice and greed that still beset him, one step removed as man actually was from the aboriginal dweller in caves and, even to this day, the victim of ignorance and fear. In contrast to this neolithic man with cigarettes and automobiles, a cliff-dweller reaching his home in an elevator, Erasmus suggested an intelligent race, well-mannered and forbearing, aware that many ways of thinking can be equally right. Hendrik was convinced himself that when men were exempt from fear they were decidedly inclined to be righteous and just, and this had been the belief of Grotius, another fellow-Dutchman, when he devised the science of international law. Hendrik has been brought up, he said, by sound Voltairians, and they had kept the tolerant spirit that had once made Holland an asylum for European thinkers of every sort. His own favourite, after Erasmus, was always Montaigne.

But the little Holland of his youth was full of small jealousies and petit-bourgeois cruelties, he wrote later, and, having means, he had come to this country to study at Harvard and Cornell with a desire to teach history before he wrote it. Then, wishing to see what he called the world of great events, he had witnessed the Russian revolution of 1906, moving from Moscow and Warsaw to Munich, where he had taken his doctor's degree in the spirit of the *Vagantes* of the Middle Ages. After he had served as a correspondent in the first world war, he could say that he had had many adventures, passing through shipwrecks and battles, fire and flood, escaping from his two *bêtes noires*, parochialism and pedantry, and ready to write the history that he knew and felt. He said it was more important to "feel" history than to know it, a statement that certain great writers would have accepted but that opened him to the taunts of smaller minds. Disliking the dull German method that alternated with propaganda,—with nationalistic flag-waving,—in this country, he realized, especially after the war, how gravely Americans needed a comprehensive view of the world's past. For he was appalled by the ignorance both of history and of Europe that led them to make such capital political blunders. But every country was turning itself into a voluntary ghetto with idiotic restrictions about crossing frontiers, and, just at the moment when people were taking to airplanes, their governments, he complained, had become oxcart-minded. Feeling that he was a hopeless realist in a world of green cheese, he attacked the "incurable vice of nationalism," and he was to write his history of this country as an episode in the development of the story of mankind. He saw himself as a pioneer of the new planetary point of view, like Nehru of the *Glimpses of World History* and H. G. Wells, who was obliged to hack down trees and blow up the stumps and lay out the land for the future. He attacked especially the cocksureness and arrogance that caused as much suffering in the present as they had caused in the past, saying that the only heresy was that which proclaimed as heretical all other modes of thinking than its own.

Hendrik's two blind spots were the Spanish and the Irish,—

he was "too terribly Dutch" to be drawn to them; and he might have said that, in any case, they were, of all peoples, the last to comprehend the Erasmian outlook. For the rest, if the upshot was that he wrote largely for children, he was none the less for all that a power over minds and even a creator of the climate of opinion that was preparing the way for a world state. Never again, thanks partly to him, could people say of India that Alexander the Great "discovered" it, as if the Indians had never discovered themselves; and he knew that the great age of exploitation had definitely come to an end, that humanity now had a collective conscience. And who could deny that he had a touch of the true historical afflatus of the writers of pre-scientific times? He carried out the idea of Bagehot that history should be like a Rembrandt etching, casting a vivid light on important causes and leaving all the rest, unseen, in shadow; and, moreover, he had the gift of storytelling that few historians any longer wish to have. He had, above all, an unshakable faith in the rise of mankind from the Protozoa, in spite of all the regressions of the world-war epoch, the mire of crime and brutal deeds into which millions of people sank as, more and more, gangsters ruled the world. He felt it was a duty of civilized man to forward the evolutionary process, believing that, through periods of growth and decline, the race was moving forward and that man was endowed with still unrealized powers. Liberal that he was, however, he did not like Rousseau, the "all-round blackguard, the contemptible bounder," nor did he like the Rousseauian schools in which he taught from time to time, regarding himself as rather a teacher than a writer. It did not please him to see boys and girls learning to "express" themselves by "hammering away at a piano with one hand and with the other eating a piece of cake."

As he grew older, Hendrik's mind turned back to Holland more and more. He recalled what Lessing said, that when the world was coming to an end he himself was going to move to Holland, for there they were always a hundred years behind the times and that would give him a new span of life. Thinking of the old Netherlands, which he said were gone for good, after the Nazi invasion, but which he remembered, he dreamed of writing a historical trilogy of the rise, the short-lived golden age and the slow decline of the country he had known as a boy. He felt that he only could do it in our language, for Pierre van Paassen was too much of a mystic for the sort of work he had in mind, and, troubled about the sub-literary style into which he sometimes fell, he hoped to be able to do it in "acceptable English." He longed, as he wrote to me, to be "the architect of a literary monument to my late native land. It seems a dignified Sir Walter Scottish way of writing the last chapter of one's own life." Meanwhile, he had bought an old Dutch house at Veere where he was to spend a number of winters and summers. He was attracted to Veere perhaps because Erasmus had known it well, and the house had fine oaken ceilings and softly purring stoves, although its walls, he added, were a little wobbly. He bought an etching-press and taught himself to etch there, and he gave Christmas parties for the children of the town. Close by he had written *R.v.R.*, while he wrote his *Lives* at Veere, summoning as "guests" the characters in what he described as "that hall of fame which everyone erects in some secret corner of his brain." His last guest was Jefferson, whom he admired in all ways and who, when his own guests had threatened to leave, sent down for another bottle of a very special port. Hendrik invited Cervantes, too, Emerson, Confucius, St. Francis, Hans Christian Andersen and dozens of others, statesmen, musicians, painters and sages, quiet workers for a decent world, one of whom was the faithful William of Orange. He ransacked old cookbooks for dishes that would please them.

It was after this small Dutch town that he named Nieuw Veere, his last Connecticut house overlooking the Sound. There he was to die in 1943, after crossing the Atlantic many times not only to old Veere but to less familiar spots that especially drew him. He had always liked small countries and felt they favoured freedom of mind, whether Switzerland or Sweden, along with Holland,—he had once lived for a while in Nietzsche's Basel; and he had a special affection for the little countries of northern Europe where he had always felt at home. It pleased him to find that in Finland all the children knew his books, and he hoped for a winter in Norway, a spring in Denmark and one more summer, at least, in Stockholm. He could sketch many parts of this loveliest of all cities, as he called it once, and in time he learned Swedish there in order to translate Bellmann's songs for a children's picture-book of this "Swedish Mozart." One summer he went to Lapland for a second visit. He wrote, "I had to have a second helping," and he found in the wilderness landscape a "suggestion of infinity," for, as he said, "a few Lapps do not count." They were so small, the Lapps, living like birds, building themselves nests wherever they went, sleeping, talking little, following their reindeer in a land that did not seem to be inhabited at all. So one felt alone there with nothing between one and the North Pole, a feeling that did queer things to the brain and set it working along unexpected lines. He had been struggling with a book which he meant to call *The Average Man,* and somehow Lapland brought it into focus. He wrote to me, "The average man is our ruler. So let me try to train him for the job, as Machiavelli tried to educate the Prince." Hendrik's idea of democracy recalled to me the critic Brownell, who had put into words my own conception of it,—"the spread in widest commonalty of aristocratic virtues." Hendrik, who cherished the notion of equality, had no taste whatever for the promiscuous equality of an undeveloped level, and, regarding himself, he once remarked, "The lower metals, like lead, melt easily, but I am not a lower metal."

Hendrik said this at a time when his vast popularity suggested Mark Twain's and his mind was almost as prodigal, impulsive and chaotic. For his abortive plans tumbled over one another. He had a dozen ideas a day, but the mortality among them was like that of our domestic shrimps, he said,—ninety-nine and a half percent of them died at birth. He planned a life of Beethoven, following his *Bach* on a larger scale, together with *The Rise and Fall of the Age of Reason,* a *Candide* in modern dress and *In Praise of Joy.* Meanwhile, he poured out other books, one of them written in a single day, with three days more for the illustrations,—he was always happier, I think, drawing than writing,—some of them Gargantuan books that were best-sellers before they appeared and that were usually translated into twenty other tongues. He sometimes even corrected his proofs by cable, while his correspondence ran to fifteen thousand letters a year and he was beset with photographers and interviewers. In order to "go on a holiday and not on a tabloid trip," he was obliged to keep his movements dark, for he was hounded by "movie people," by "serial people," by "syndicate people" and could not escape *pourparlers* with Hollywood and Hearst. (Though, regarding Hollywood, he spoke the truth when he said, "I understand more about what goes on in Lhasa.") Knighted by the Dutch queen and a guest at the White House, he was always deep in public causes, while he continually reminded himself of the old Buddhist law,

"The holy man does not leave his shrine." To me he wrote, "Farewell to the multitude and back to the wooden tower of Old Greenwich." No use! He could not retire from the battle with Hitler, and with many other victims of the jazz age he was to die early of over-excitement.

Like Mark Twain in certain ways, Hendrik had been all the more so in the triumphal progress of his cruise around the world when, as a guest of the steamship company, he addressed the travellers as he lectured in Hawaii and New Zealand, Zanzibar and Capetown. He found that almost every man, woman and child he encountered had, at one time or another, read one of his books, while he discovered that everywhere the world was dominated by what he described as "the old master magicians." Whether in Polynesia or the Buddhist, the Moslem or the Christian lands, he saw misery caused by a "lack of rational thinking," by "magic" in the hands of the old who were supposedly wise and who kept the young in their places. Meanwhile, "the young men, grown to manhood, find that their comfort and ease depend upon the continued belief in magic,—and so it goes on, world without end and without end of misery." Hendrik continued, "I want for heroes reasonable Erasmian men who understand that this world, while it may never be perfect, could easily be made more agreeable."

As one who loved what Lytton Strachey called "clean brevity," I could not think of Hendrik as an important writer, but he was a bright symbol of a still expansive time that seemed already remote before his death. What he called magic had won the day and there was no room for Erasmian men among writers who abhorred liberal humanism, who felt, with Kierkegaard, that earthly happiness is a sin and that the idea of progress is an infantile illusion. In the new day Comte's belief that the true aim of art is to "charm and ameliorate humanity" had utterly vanished, along with all the notions of the age of reason. But the question was still to be entertained whether the ideas that Hendrik held were nineteenth-century deceits and contemptible fables or whether in the long run they would not prove to be necessary if the human race was to survive and grow. Hendrik, all-curious, compassionate, humane, was one of the lieutenants in the pilgrimage of humanity up from the cavemen, and, for the rest, there were few in our time who so enabled one to share what Burckhardt called the "banquet" of the art of the past.

## CHAPTER X

# A HAMLET OF TEN HOUSES

NEAR THE up-state road towards Albany, two or three hours from New York, Joel Spingarn lived in a sheltered valley, or, rather, he summered at Troutbeck in a picturesque, spreading, ample house surrounded with lawns, old oaks, rivulets and gardens. His domain was a private park that was planted with rare shrubs and trees, many of them brought from the Arnold Arboretum, where Joel had been a friend of the great Charles Sargent, with a rose garden, a sunken garden, terraces, greenhouses, trellises to support the multiform clematis that was Joel's delight. His collection of more than two hundred varieties of this flowering climber was renowned in the world of horticulture.

Troutbeck had long been connected with writers and writing. In two old dwellings on the place the literary farmers, the Bentons, had lived, correspondents of Thoreau, hosts of Greeley, and the Brotherhood of the New Life of Thomas Lake Harris had also flourished in Amenia sixty years before. By Joel's well John Burroughs had first read *Leaves of Grass*,— the old farm was redolent of Whitman and Emerson also, about whom one of the Bentons had written a book; while Joel himself contributed a note to the "Newness" of our time that in some ways recalled to me the old one. For as one who introduced the contemporary thinking of Italy, he too was a light-bringer of new learning. Troutbeck, moreover, suggested the kind of English country-house that had once brought together philosophers and poets and fostered the literary life and the development of thought; and there was a time, in fact, when Joel hoped to make the valley a home for the muses. He owned what Lewis Mumford called a "hamlet of ten houses,"—the hamlet of the Chinese poets,—adjoining Trout-beck; and, renovating these, he turned them over to literary friends who also came to spend the summer there.

Among the friends who occupied these cottages from time to time were Walter and Magda Pach, the Lewis Mumfords and Geroid Tanqueray Robinson, one of our *Freeman* editors and a great student of Russian rural life. It was easy for me to drive over from Westport to this umbrageous valley where in the summer months good talk abounded, where Ernest Boyd too was a visitor and Lewis and Sophy Mumford presently bought the house where they lived henceforward. Somewhat older than the rest of us, Joel Spingarn might have been called the guardian or incarnation of the *genius loci*, proud, shy, cordial and winning as he was, with a distinctly Italianate air as of some Ferrarese courtier of the days of Tasso. There was a kind of inevitability in the name "De Fiori" that Lewis, in a fictional dialogue, bestowed upon him, for he had more than a touch of the style and manner of certain Italian coteries of the later Renaissance. I wondered if this was not partly the fruit of his early study of the *Galateo*, the *Cortigiano* and other old courtesy books, for in his youth he had steeped himself in the history of chivalric ideals and their evolution from the Romans and the Middle Ages. But there was no suggestion of the exotic in him. For all its aesthetic overtones, his manner was quite natural, and he was really charming like some of his poems, unpretentious poems that were sometimes courtly too in their gallantry and nobility of feeling.

What seemed to me the Italianate note in Joel's personality was definitely marked in his thinking, in the form of his mind, for long before he had written his history of criticism in the Renaissance he had gone to school to the modern Italians also. That book introduced him to Croce, of whom he became an apostle, and, forwarding Croce's ideas at home, with those of Francesco De Sanctis, he hoped to win over Americans to their mode of thought. He would have liked to put an end to the current American jargon that was drawn from psychology, sociology, biology, economics, replacing it with the ideality of the Italian nomenclature, faith, freedom, the spirituality of culture and so on. As early as 1910 he had written *The New Criticism,* a name that was later revived by the school of critics who carried on, substantially, though without credit to him, a critical vein that he had opened up. For the task of the critic, in his view, was to state the intention of the poet and ascertain how far he had fulfilled it, ignoring all questions of value in the study of expression, and the work of the later "new critics," devoted to formal analysis, excluding all other interests, exemplified this. It seemed to be only as an afterthought that he asked the further question, Is what the poet expresses worth expressing?—a question he no more dwelt upon than the "close" critics who followed him in taking for granted everything but expression itself.

All this had its piquancy at a time when American critics were obsessed with what Joel described as "practical wisdom,"—concerns that were psychological, historical and social,—scarcely ever brooding over the meaning of art with the sort of discreet reverence that it properly merits. As for the rest, there was much to be said for the work of Joel's followers, in spite of all

one had to say against it, for it tightened the bolts and screws
of American writing; and in any case, in his general essays,
Joel himself went far beyond the narrow textual interests of
many of them. While his specific critical theory seemed to me
sterile and thin,—"as brittle as spun glass," Lewis Mumford
called it,—he was in other ways a moving spirit, aware as he
was that the new literature rising all about us called as well for
social criticism. He had been excited by the Armory Show, of
which our friend Walter Pach had been to a certain extent
the originating spirit, and at that time he had hoped that
American writers would follow the painters in their "divine
release from custom and convention." For in 1913, measured
by their courage, our poetry and fiction had seemed pusillani-
mous and timid,—anæmic, as Joel felt, academic and faded,—
and he held up to ridicule the dry rot of the time with its
decayed traditions of Victorian England. He never tired of
saying that in art all depends on what Keats called a "fine
excess." Attacking in the same breath the specialization of
scholarship that copied the vices of the Germans instead of
their virtues, he spoke for pluck and freedom in this realm
also, and he had lost his professorate as a result of protesting
against the removal and ruin of a fellow-scholar. Everyone
knew and quoted his lines about the "slayer in scarlet" and
the faint-hearted faculty that huddled round him; and, defending his dishonoured friend in *The Fate of a Scholar*, he
appealed for the high heart in the teacher's world. Joel's key-
word was "creative," a word that savoured of the time and
one he applied also to connoisseurship, noting how negative
and colourless our Medicis were in the field of taste when they
were so dynamic in the field of action.

Eager as Joel was, however, to forward an American renaissance, he was by no means sure of its ultimate triumph, and

he could see no reason to suppose that our national energy would flower in the great literature that many of us hoped for. In his heart I think he felt that the United States would end as a still more infertile replica of Rome, a semi-barbarian empire, culturally weak, tutored by the English as the Romans had been tutored by the Greeks. But he enjoyed the stir of the expanding moment, using his own reviews in *The Freeman* to clear up critical problems that had been misunderstood, as he thought, by others. As a kind of partner in a publishing house, in his "European Library," he brought out books by Croce and his friend Gentile, by Remy de Gourmont and G. A. Borgese, with Goethe's literary essays and new Italian, German and Spanish novels. I spent many hours with him in his greenhouses and gardens or in the splendid library, with its casement windows and walls of books, that witnessed a sort of symposium now and then. I remember one of these on the pros and cons of censorship, though who the speakers were I cannot remember; but in *Aesthetics: a Dialogue* Lewis Mumford recorded another that took place in 1921. This was printed as a "Troutbeck Leaflet," one of a series of little brochures that Joel brought out from time to time with essays of E. A. Robinson, Sinclair Lewis, the poet G. E. Woodberry and two or three others. On this occasion Ernest Boyd, Joel, Lewis and I myself discussed our various ideas of criticism.

I do not connect Walter Pach with these conversazioni,—he spent few summers in the valley,—but I already knew him well and often went for walks with him at Troutbeck as in Greenwich Village and Westport later. Walter did not love the country as Joel and Lewis loved it,—he could never have written a book like *Green Memories,* for instance, in which Lewis poured out his affection for the rural scene; for he was a born metropolitan, a lover of city streets and sights who only put up with the country for the sake of the landscape. I think the greenness of the trees meant more to him than the trees themselves,—he had a special relish, as a painter, for green; and he built his little stone cottage at Brewster mainly to please Magda, who loved to paint the flowers she cultivated there. Magda, who had grown up in Dresden, a German of the heroic type, might have been a model for Dürer painting the Madonna, and Walter, a child of the Pach photographers who had invented the wet plate, had certain German characteristics also. He looked, with his drooping hussar's moustache, like a milder contemplative Nietzsche, and his astonishing saturation in the history of art and in art itself reminded one of a German professor of aesthetics. But his humour was American and at any moment he would drop into a broad Yankee manner of speech that savoured of the brothers Prendergast. He was full of anecdotes of his Western lecturing tours at the girls' college, for instance, where the students in a body petitioned the president to remove from their parlour a cast of the Venus de Milo because it aroused impure thoughts in the visiting boys. I wondered if some of the visiting boys had not become the novelists of whom we knew so many in our time and whose thoughts might have been obsessively impure because so many of the girls had been so prudish.

It was through Walter that I had met the Prendergasts when they were still living in New York, on the south side of Washington Square, a remnant of the old Knickerbocker town where Walter himself was to live in coming years. He and Magda told many tales about these childlike brothers, exquisite artists both and most lovable men, whom one day Magda promised a bowl of pea-soup and was then delayed in carrying it round to them. When she opened their door at last, she found them sitting at the board, each with a spoon upraised

in a hopeful hand, like a pair of fledgling robins waiting in
the nest, a scene that evoked for me the nature of these
brothers, as idyllically unworldly as painting monks might be.
All the stories that Charles told me after his elder brother's
death recalled the fathomless innocence of this happy painter
whom I always thought of, because of this trait and his beautiful feeling for colour, as a sort of Yankee Fra Angelico. Walter
had recognized at once the quality of Maurice Prendergast, the
first American artist to be aware of Cézanne, "old Paul," as
Prendergast called him, regarding whom Walter himself had
been one of the first Americans to write an essay.

In our time of discovery at home, Walter was one of the
first, moreover, to appreciate the "grand provincial," Thomas
Eakins, and he had persuaded the Louvre to buy one of the
pictures that filled the painter's dark old Philadelphia house.
He had known Eakins and, more intimately, Ryder, whom
he had visited often in the cave in the slums where this visionary lived in his own dream-world, slowly emerging in the
general mind, oblivious as he was to this, at the moment when
Herman Melville was also emerging. In college I had never
heard Melville mentioned, and although I had read him in
California two or three years later many of my friends were
unaware of him. He was not generally known, I think, before
the South Seas became a vogue or before Raymond Weaver
wrote his life. I remember that even quite late in the twenties,
when Lewis Mumford undertook to write his biography of
Melville, one of the granddaughters of the great man, who was
later so helpful to students, was surprised that people were
showing an interest in him. She had been aware of him only
as a strange old soul whom no one had ever regarded as a person of importance,—"grim as a chimney when the house is
gone," as Lewis wrote in one of his own poems; while now all

the young looked at each other with a wild surmise as this new planet swam into their ken.

In the fiercely competitive world of the twenties, Walter never received his due as a missionary, so to put it, of the modern painting that was disjoined, as many thought, from the main body of art, which in its length and breadth he knew so fully. He was at home in all epochs and schools from the high days of Egypt, the Chinese, the Greeks, the Aztecs and the Mayans, and he saw no dichotomy between the work of any of them and that of the sculptors and painters he had encountered in Paris. In short, his deep sense of tradition involved an unwavering faith that his "masters of modern art" continued it, and it was with this belief that he played so large a role in choosing for the Armory Show the French sculptures and pictures. If, in the history of American art, this show was the great divide, he, more than anyone else, was responsible for it; for what could Arthur B. Davies have chosen to represent the new age in France if Walter had not for years been living there? He had known, really known, when they were still the wild beasts, Rouault, Braque, Derain, Brancusi, Picasso, and earlier still he had had long talks with Renoir and visited Claude Monet at Giverny. When only a handful of people at home were aware of the post-impressionists, he had steeped himself already in their work, and he had written about all these men, while Matisse had made a portrait etching of him. He, more than anyone else, contributed to select this work, which caused such a revolution in the New York art world at a time when American museums were filled with the pictures that Walter himself denounced in *Ananias, or the False Artist.*

Others, of course, wrote admirably about the modern art of which he knew so well the arterial structure, the nerves, the bones and the flesh as well as the soul; but what distinguished

Walter was the sense of continuity with which he understood
its heredity also. He was enchanted equally by the present and
the past, a feeling that he shared with some of the great art-
critics he knew, especially Roger Fry and Meier-Graefe, and
this enabled him to organize so finely the exhibition for the
World's Fair later. Meanwhile, he and Magda conducted the
annual Independents' show, and he responded early,—in 1922,
—to the intellectual ferment in Mexico City. There, for the first
time, he felt what Waldo Frank had felt, that the New World
was no longer an aspiration but an actual, spiritual and even
a visible fact, for New York seemed a mere prolongation of
London and Paris beside Mexico City in revolution. In Mexico,
as Walter felt and as he wrote to me, there was more new life
apparently than there was in Russia, and he sent me the
superb magazines that were symbols of the Mexican renaissance
in writing, painting, education, music and dancing. The Mexicans were restoring the old pyramids and temples of the pre-
Spanish autochthonous culture also. Walter made friends not
only with Alfonso Reyes and Juan Larrea, whom I was to meet
presently in New York, but with the great painters Orozco
and Diego Rivera whose work was something new under the
sun. Orozco, whose large pictures were still to come and who
was known at the time simply as the cartoonist of the revolution, regularly came to Walter's university classes, while, with
Siqueiros and Rivera, he was evolving a powerful, original,
indigenous Mexican style. No influence from the outside
seemed greatly to affect these painters, although Giotto and
obviously Cézanne had interested Rivera, whom one of Walter's letters had sent to Paris. Rivera had gone as a young man
to Madrid and a letter of Walter's to one of his friends begged
him not to waste time there since the whole contemporary
movement was across the French border. Fifteen years later, in

Mexico, Rivera told Walter how much he owed, he and his friend, to the phrases of an unknown man.

Both then and twenty years afterwards Walter delighted in Mexico, in the stir of the moment there, in the Aztec artifacts he brought back and in a certain monastery where he found sixteenth-century frescoes by a painter who had studied Michelangelo. "The old Mexicans, always intelligent, went to headquarters," he wrote to me, but their new school went nowhere, or virtually nowhere, and owed little to Italy, Spain or France. When, in the early thirties, Diego Rivera was in New York, painting for a down-town school a series of frescoes, I had a feeling, as I watched him working there, that was entirely new in my experience of painters. Walter's and my old friend John Sloan thought he was the greatest American painter and the only one who belonged with the old masters; but, while the scene took one back to some atelier of the Renaissance, there was something that had no precedent in the scene and the man. Crouching on the platform, smiling as he painted, he suggested a burlier Giotto at work on a fresco, but there was an element in him as far removed from the European as if he had been a Hindu or a Chinese; and this was the Mexican Indian note at a pitch that had never been known before and that seemed somehow profoundly American also. I was at that time planning my New England books, and I was struck by his masterly heads of Thoreau and Emerson of which he gave me photographs with cordial inscriptions. He seemed to know these characters by intuition. But he had also read them, for he was a great reader. Walter quoted to him a phrase from Milton's *Areopagitica* and Rivera took up the quotation and completed it in English.

It was to Walter that I owed my meeting with Rivera, and how many other occasions I had to be grateful to this friend

who was always at leisure for walks, for talks, for letters. He
had time for anyone who shared his own feeling for art,
whether new work or the pictures that, as he once said to me,
"We have known all our lives and never know." He liked to
quote Renoir's remark to him when he had asked the great old
man how best to become an artist,—"In the Museum!"—and I
could scarcely count the times I was to visit museums with
him, whether in New York or in Paris, first or last. It was in
the Metropolitan, near which he had grown up and while he
was copying there and still in the art school, that he had
overheard William M. Chase describe Manet's "Boy with the
Sword" as the only picture in the room that could be hung
with the old masters. That was in the day when Bouguereau
reigned still, before Duveen waved his wand over American
collectors, and Walter, awakened, had gone to Spain in charge
of Chase's pupils, painting himself and remaining in Europe
to study. Jo Davidson, who was in Spain at the time, told me
that one could pick up there even a large El Greco for fifty
dollars. Jo himself had settled in France in the lovely old house
on the river Indre from which he had come to London, where
I first met him; and Walter too, living in Paris, had acquired,
like Jo, an almost religious feeling for the art of the French.
Jo never again could feel at home in the wooden New England
villages that came to possess for me a special charm, while I
always felt that, in his heart of hearts, Walter could not quite
believe that a modern picture *not* French could be the real
right thing. I mean it could not be "one of the supreme things,"
—Walter's own phrase,—and no doubt he was right for the
hundred years since Delacroix and Ingres, true as it was that,
in our own small world, he recognized so lovingly Copley and
Eakins, Prendergast and Ryder. If one could single out any
painters who were passions with him, they would be Ingres,

whose life he wrote, Delacroix, whom he translated, and Géri-
cault, of whom he owned two or three examples. He had two
Delacroix water-colours, and I remember a day when he stood
beside one for half an hour, never uttering twice a phrase or
a thought. With every word he revealed some new scrap of
meaning or fresh nuance, and I might have been a child hearing his first fairy-story. For such gifts of demonstration were
altogether new to me. Walter freely took his way through the
underground caverns that no one ever penetrates in the usual
art books.

I always supposed that Winckelmann was rather like Walter,
who might so easily have been himself the learned curator of
pictures and books at some eighteenth-century German grand-
ducal court. What made him so engaging was a constant sense
of the enchantment of art, a discriminating quiet excitement
that never lost its bloom, a feeling that if all men could share
his pleasure in these wonderfully beautiful things the world
would find itself redeemed from evil. He wrote me once to ask
if I knew Copley's letters, really surprising letters that he had
just found; then he wrote to say that I must see the pictures
of John Quidor, a forgotten New York painter who had come
to light. Did I know, moreover, the fine passage in *Don
Quixote* in which the Canon of Toledo discusses books? He
took me to see Joseph Brummer, the clairvoyant dealer, who
could touch in the dark any fragment of sculpture in basalt or
in marble and instantly tell you its provenance in Egypt or
Greece. Or in Burma, Roman Spain or Guatemala. Once
Walter repeated a remark of the daughter of his friend Elie
Faure, whose five-volume *History of Art* he translated, one
that pleased me because I had spent a good part of a week
trying to put into English one of Faure's essays. It was a long
paper for *The Freeman* about Charlie Chaplin, and there

were murky passages in both instalments that I could make neither head nor tail of. So I understood what Faure's daughter meant when she said, "O Papa, I've read such good news in the paper. Elie Faure's books are going to be translated into French."

But, to go back to Troutbeck and the hamlet of ten houses that sheltered in the twenties so many of our friends, I was to know it well for many years to come, sometimes visiting the Spingarns, sometimes the Mumfords. Lewis would come out early for the spring planting, for, with his broccoli, lettuce and beets, he was never more himself there than when he was delving in the earth. He was a lover of lilacs too and the Mackintosh apples in his orchard on a warm September afternoon; and he was a great walker in the woods looking for the first hepatica, the first ripe wild strawberries and the first bloodroot. With Sophy and Geddes, the little boy who was named for the Scottish philosopher, Lewis's own master before the twenties, he noted the first mild night when the frogs burst forth in spring and the day when the red-winged blackbird first rose from the swamp. All three paid daily visits to the buckeye tree to watch its great candles unfolding, and they were to know the year-round span of country life when they spent winters also in the valley. Lewis's deep feeling for the rural scene explained his defence of regionalism against the encroachments of the city,—against the megalopolitan view of life,—as it also explained his understanding of the world of Emerson and Thoreau which, in *The Golden Day,* he presented so finely. Never sharing my negative views of certain of our old writers, he had seen three or four as true world figures, anticipating D. H. Lawrence's notion of them as going in some ways further than any Europeans.

Of all my writing contemporaries, Lewis Mumford was

always the one with whom I felt most sympathetic and closely allied, and from the moment I fell in with him he took for me the place that Randolph Bourne's death had left vacant. I had a fraternal feeling for him that steadily grew with the years, and I connected this with a remark of William James in a letter to his friend Josiah Royce: "In converse with you I have always felt that my life was being lived importantly." It was not that he flattered my vanity,—quite the reverse,—but that in certain respects he enhanced my life, for, sharing some of my beliefs, he so expressed them in his own way that they came back to me with redoubled value. There was nothing of my own thought in his, and his interests were different from mine,—he lived in many worlds I scarcely entered; but there was much in his feeling for life that raised my own to a higher power and the consciousness that he existed nourished me. His monolithic integrity excited and touched me, his gift of keeping life essentially simple, his savage indignation, so rare in our fatalistic time, even his ability to loaf and invite the soul. For, unhasting and unresting, he had this in common with the sages of Diogenes Laertius and our own Walden. Then he had the qualities that Burckhardt called the outstanding traits of all great men,—plenitude and single-mindedness,— with the Palagian optimism that was our one great tradition, summed up in the maxim, "If I ought, I can." In a time that was more and more oppressed with a sense of the vanity of the human will, he was constantly aware of our still untapped resources; his key-word was always "renewal"; and, with all his feeling for the past, he cared less for what *has been* than for what *may be.* Lewis was one of the few men who have not *ideas* but *an idea,* and he was to spend his life working this out.

When I first met him in 1920, he had just returned from

London in the spirit of so many others of my generation who
had been, as it were, converted to the idea of a life at home
after living, or wishing to live, in England or Europe. Lewis
himself often said that by natural sympathy and education
he somehow felt closer to the men of my time than to his own
contemporaries who were ten years younger, the leaders of the
lost generation, disillusioned romantics like Wilson, Fitzgerald,
Dos Passos, Hemingway and Cummings. Actually of the age
of these, he had matured in the confident years, the so-called
innocent years of the pre-war epoch when soldiers were only
tin soldiers, as he said in a letter,—with a liking for brass but-
tons, music and drums,—and it was his distinction never to lose
their confidence and hope while fully sharing the later consciousness of evil. He had caught in England the last rays of
the morning glow of William Morris's poetic socialism, and he
was to remain a vitalist in a world of mechanists, behaviourists,
determinists, Marxians and so on. In London, still virtually
a boy, he had been managing editor of the *Sociological Review,* and Sir Patrick Geddes, with whom he worked, urged
Lewis to go to Palestine and plan the new Jerusalem with him
there. Lewis, convinced that "old stocks may rove" while "pioneers must settle down," thanked Geddes for a thousand
thoughts to be tended and developed, but said he must set
them out in an American garden, and, returning to America,
he began walking through the streets and planning with a
new purpose excursions beyond them. Geddes, of whom I myself had a glimpse later in New York,—in a restaurant near the
New School, at a table in a corner,—had shown Lewis how to
interpret cities, their place in civilization, their origins, their
growth, their import for human living. Looking into the past,
examining the present and sketching a future for the general
scene that would best serve the interests of human renewal,

Lewis, whose first book had been *The Story of Utopias,* studied city planning and architecture. He had been for a while a surveyor, and he made friends with community planners, architects, geographers, engineers. Lewis had begun with the human setting before he went on to explore education, aesthetics, ethics and the conduct of life, but, starting with the body of civilization, he was concerned with this only as the outward and visible garment of its heart and soul.

Like Randolph Bourne before him, Lewis was a capital letter-writer, one of the few in a period when novelists and poets were sometimes known never to write letters at all. Like Bourne again, he fought against the cultural humility that had led us to ignore the American past, beginning with what he once described as the pathless waste of our architecture before he wrote *Sticks and Stones* in 1924. In this he revived much that was unknown or forgotten, and he taught thousands to look at banks and at business buildings and railroad stations who had never given these a glance before. It had not occurred to them that such things could be architecture, and Lewis opened a large field here when others were discovering American antiques, American primitives, American folk art and so on. It was he who made household words of the names of Roebling of the Brooklyn Bridge, Richardson, Louis Sullivan and Frank Lloyd Wright, of whom he wrote so admirably in *The South in Architecture, From the Ground Up* and other books. Only when he had written of them did we fully realize that America had native master-builders, and one read these books with some of the excitement that people had found in Audubon's birds or Asa Gray's discovery of the American flora.

In *The Brown Decades,* moreover, Lewis discovered the generation just before our own, a period so close to ourselves that we had never seen it, as he discovered much of the present in the yearbook that he edited with Paul Rosenfeld, Alfred Kreymborg and, briefly, myself. I mean the present of the twenties and thirties that appeared in *The American Caravan,* a publication which first brought out many writers, at the time unknown, solitary, stranded and what not, who were famous later. For Lewis, like William James, whom he admired, was always in touch with the young and followed them sympathetically through decade after decade, understanding their spiritual plight after two world wars that virtually destroyed their faith in the future of man. Born as he said he had been himself into the cocky pre-war world, he fully realized nevertheless why the young became so grave while only the old, in the later time, were giddy. He knew that the optimists of the machine had forgotten that there was madness and night and that mankind had mystery to contend with, coëxisting with universal literacy, science and daylight, and why, because they ignored the darker side of the nature of man, they had been unprepared for the catastrophe that followed. He could see why it was that a grimly senescent youth confronted the still youthful senescents of the older generation, and having, along with Emerson and Whitman, read Pascal and Saint Augustine, he was fully able to enter their state of mind. Writers like Melville and Dostoievsky, with their sense of the presence of evil, had fitted him to grasp the post-war scene, the disintegrated world in which humankind, convinced of its inadequacy, ceased to believe in its own powers of self-renewal.

No one else whom I knew was more aware than Lewis of all that was dark and tragic in the post-war time, and what made him unique was that, understanding this, he retained the energy and faith of the time before it. He kept, in a broken world, the sense of wholeness, and he had none of the fatalism of so many younger minds under the mounting threat of atomic destruction. The notion of destruction involved for him the notion of renewal, disintegration implied reintegration, and what concerned him chiefly was to "create soil again" in a civilization "denuded to the bare rock." For him the resources of humankind were still inexhaustible, requiring only the sense of a new purpose and direction; and, with his feeling for the inner life, he was convinced that the problem of our time was to restore the lost respect for this. For Western man had forgotten it in his concentration on the improvement of the machine. In a world obsessed with determinism, the human person must come back to the centre of the stage, he said, as actor and hero, summoning the forces of life to take part in a new drama; and he saw signs of the approach of spring and a deeper faith for living in the dark winter of the present.

I am speaking here of the forties and fifties, but all this might have been seen already in the Lewis I had known twenty years before.

## CHAPTER XI

# THIRTY AGAINST AMERICA

IT WAS during the early nineteen-twenties that the word "expatriate" came into play,—although there was nothing new in expatriation,—a word that suggested in later times the flight of young writers from the country of which they felt that they were the *avant-garde*. (Another word that savoured of the moment.) Anywhere, anywhere out of the world, out of the dull American world, was a general cry among those who had returned from the war and who wished never to go back to the Tilbury Towns of their childhood, the Winesburgs, the Spoon Rivers or the Gopher Prairies. In one publishing house or another I had read a manuscript every day by some young person born in some such town who felt that he was too sensitive for these crude surroundings and who said good-bye to Wisconsin, Ohio or Kansas. One and all were obsessed with the problem of the artist in America,—"ever an outcast, a pariah," Henry Miller said,—and with what they considered the sterility of the American scene; and they usually agreed with Samuel Butler that America was "the last place" in which life was "endurable at all for an inspired writer."

There were those who were drawn to the primitive, to the islands that attracted my brother-in-law, especially at this moment when the fame of Melville had just begun to rise in the general mind. For others, like Carl van Vechten, the

Harlem of the Negroes had a similar charm; and there was William Seabrook, who said he had always been running away to deserts and to voodoo temples and to jungles. A few set out for Mexico, John Reed, for instance, for a while, and Katharine Anne Porter, who was writing stories, at a time when Mexican furniture and glass were spreading across the Rio Grande and Mexican art was rising with Rivera and Orozco. Like many another, John Sloan pitched a new tent in Santa Fe. "What a marvellous place the Southwest is for the New Yorker to fall upon," Waldo Frank had written in one of his letters, "with its double layer of Indian and Hispanic cultures, lying there, rotting and rich under the low sun." Waldo had found in the sacred Kiva to which he was admitted "a great incentive to new vision and stronger wisdom"; and in the Indian ceremonials many discovered something real they had never felt in the rituals and ceremonials of home. Near by, at Taos, Mabel Dodge, rejecting "the false new America in the East," traced the "true" America in "the Indian blood stream," while D. H. Lawrence, escaping from a Europe to which so many were eager to go, exclaimed, "To your tents, O America. Listen to your own." He too meant by "your own" the dusky red men.

It was to Europe, and mainly to Paris, that most were determined to find their way, oddly enough in the spirit of Montaigne when he said he had also gone abroad "from a lack of relation to the present conditions of our country." An English visitor in New York remarked to a friend of mine that he could not understand this general hegira: the young Americans whom he saw seemed to be always asking him if he knew of any job they could get in Europe. Why were so many young men swarming to France? A vigorous nation sending its best to a dying civilization, youth rushing to live with senility, —how did this happen? Albert Nock, who had lived in Europe quietly for many years, explained the stampede as part of the "desperation" that characterized young writers during these years, a strange spirit that seemed to rest on a whole generation of young men who were apparently bent on self-destruction. They all reminded him of Turgenev's Misha, generous and truthful, not depraved but wretchedly dissatisfied and giving themselves up, unhappy as they were, for "lost." Regarding this generation, Nock used the same word as Gertrude Stein, of whom he knew nothing at the moment; nor was he aware that this desperation was to give rise to the religion of art that was to thrive in the twenties, especially in Paris. For when so much had been swept away that had made life worth living,— the faith in human goodness, security, tradition,—art, form, colour, craftsmanship was something to cling to, something solid and real in a world of ruin. So it was no wonder, in this feverish decade, that good writing flourished like a prairie fire in a high wind. Meanwhile, as one of the young men said, "There is something the matter with a culture whose youth is eager to desert it . . . Rebellious youth is not wanted here, the imaginative and adventurous and artistically creative"; and he asked, in *The Freeman*, "What can a young man do?"

As Ezra Pound said later, most of these young men left "in disgust," not in the mood of the earlier seekers of culture; and the most talked about of the exiles of 1921 was the writer of this manifesto, Harold Stearns. Only a few months before, I had worked with him and a group of our friends, in Jones Street in Greenwich Village, on the symposium, *Civilization in the United States,* discussing various aspects of American culture. Nock must have had Harold Stearns in mind when he spoke of François Villon as one of the prototypes of the lost generation, for there was an element in Harold Stearns of the mediæval vagabond student who is known, in contemporary parlance, as the literary bum. As everyone knew, he figured soon in *The Sun Also Rises* as the "small, heavy, slow" Harvey Stone who seemed to be always sitting outside the Dôme or the Rotonde with a pile of saucers in front of him, needing a shave. Then, having had "nothing to eat for five days," he would reappear and "go off like a cat . . . pretty sad," a tale he told in his autobiography in which he said the wind always "blew coldest down the street I know." Hemingway bought clothes for him and the ever-to-be-blessed Jo Davidson found a job for him on the Paris *Herald,* while, longing to write about Rabelais the book that Nock actually wrote, he turned out racing stories for sporting papers. For he shared Sherwood Anderson's feeling for horses and the race-track. He wrote to me, "I do not expect ever to come back. I'm leaving Paris when they carry me out"; and he also wrote, "You know for some reason I gather myths about myself as easily as a snowball gathers snow rolling down a hill." In fact, he lived almost to become a myth, "broke and bitter, poor and alone," as he said in *The Street I Know,* "without a friend or a woman to keep me," sleeping on benches on the boulevards in a Paris that became for him, like his New York, a city of dreadful night. At the moment, George Orwell too was down and out there.

Thirteen years were to pass before Harold Stearns came home again, like Melville's Israel Potter, a stranger in a strange land, without clothes or a trunk or a dime, without so much as a packet of cigarettes. Meanwhile, others with happier fortunes turned Montparnasse into a sort of transplanted Greenwich Village, sometimes discovering a talent in themselves with which to return to a native scene that was little to their taste but that usually obsessed them. For, expatriates as they might be, they almost invariably wrote about the "half savage country, out of date," to which Ezra Pound referred in his finest poem, and they were "always attempting to formulate an attitude toward life in the United States," like the hero of Edmund Wilson's *I Thought of Daisy*. "Discovering" or "rediscovering" America might have been called their métier at this time when even an essay on Alfred Stieglitz began with a psychological history of the country and when the discussion of any theme seemed to involve first or last a new theory of America, the American character or what not. They were as full of their country as the Spaniards were of Spain or as the Poles were of the "Polish question," while their great aim was to escape from the "moral obligation to be optimistic" and from "Protestant morality" and "success" in American terms. "What do you think of Mencken?" was a universal question; and, knowing little of the past of American writing, they were not interested in the past of Europe either. They had seldom read any American books but *Moby-Dick* and *Huckleberry Finn*. Rejecting English writers almost by instinct, as a matter of course,—the English who had overawed their predecessors,— they read the Russian novelists and especially the French, and, among these, particularly, Flaubert. For Flaubert shared their contempt for the philistines and the business men of whom they had seen too much at home.

Well I had known, a few years before, in Paris but mainly in London, that old excitement, for Americans, of the European scene which all but suggested the sensation of life as somehow multiplied tenfold that epileptics experience before their attacks. It was easy to understand the mood of the newcomers in Paris "where everybody felt at home," as one of them said, a *patrie* of the imagination that preëxisted in the memory as it were and as even Jefferson and Franklin might have felt. Vincent Sheean, who said this, remarked that his voyage thither had been like the voyage of the "Santa Maria" in reverse,—the correspondent whose distinction was that he could feel as history the events he was living and observing. Like others from the Middle West who made literary history in Paris, Sheean seemed to have been born a man of the world, and this was a note that characterized the new men who were so unlike the consciously provincial men of old. The exiles of the twenties were prepared to believe the asseveration of Gertrude Stein that Americans were "creating" the new century which the English were "refusing,"—because the twentieth century was "too many" for the English,—a statement that Ezra Pound confirmed when he claimed for Americans virtually all the twentieth-century developments in English verse.

Meanwhile, for American writers, there had never been a time and place so favourable to literary growth,—that is to say, to their technical growth, to the rise of the artist in them,—at a time when artists were looked upon as heroes. For in that nihilistic air the reverence that religion had once absorbed was redirected towards artists, who were regarded as saints, the craftsmen who had maintained their integrity, who had remained inviolate in a world that seemed to be generally tumbling to pieces. There had never been anything quite like the feeling that came to invest for a long generation the literary heroes Mallarmé, Flaubert, Proust, Joyce, Henry James and a few others,—the literary martyrology of the post-war epoch,—a reverence that aroused in the young a spirit of emulation such as real saints have aroused in ages of faith. In a Paris, moreover, where art itself was actively present in the general mind and where every café table and hotel bedroom brought back the name of some great writer, they found exciting teachers in the art of writing who were devoted to the problems of literary form. Beyond even Pound and Gertrude Stein, there was Ford Madox Ford, an Englishman who had found for himself that "to be in touch with youth" was a necessity if he was to write. Ford, temperamentally drawn to the literary army from the Middle West and fully conscious of the stirring of aesthetic life there, felt that the next great literary movement had been predestined to come from there because it had been scarcely touched by the world war. It was the one great tract in the Western world that was still virgin soil for the literary spirit.

Together with the problems of literary art, the art of living was paramount in most of these disaffected American minds, and, constantly comparing the scenes they remembered with all they found in Paris, they could not contain their scorn of the world at home. They were generally convinced that Mencken was right in picturing the United States as a fool's country of boobery and buncombe, and they censured virtually everything in the land they had come from, while, as a rule, they continued to write about it. They "disposed of California scenery," as Sinclair Lewis's Dodsworth said, after he had listened to their talk at café tables, of "the institution of marriage" as well, "Whistler, corn fritters and President Wilson," along with "the use of catsup" and "cement roads." They denounced the tradesmen at home who made soap and motor-cars "instead of collecting old lace," as Dodsworth put it, while they checked up their own profitable holdings in soap and motor-cars, the holdings that enabled them to be "so disposive." There was in fact another way of looking at many American things, and European things also, as others were to feel, when many of the complaints of the twenties came to seem foolish. But it was still more foolish later to condemn the rebels of that day, considering how much of their folly proved to be tonic.

What, later, called for an explanation was the strange unanimity with which a whole generation turned against the country, or at least a large part of the generation that had experienced the first world war, with a few who had begun to write before it. For in this fruit of the *zeitgeist*, in this general dispraise of the "American way," there was nothing conspiratorial, there was no collusion, or even, aside from the group who wrote *Civilization in the United States*, no round-up for the purpose of talking it over. Yet novelists and poets, playwrights and critics from every corner of the country seemed to see mainly the negative in the "jungle," in the "maelstrom," in the complacent, the uniquely dull, the money-ridden land they knew, the only land, they felt, in which artists were flouted. They were like the Russian nihilists of old who, in their time of negation, found scarcely anything worth saving in their country and who said, "What can be broken, we shall break. Smash right and left,"—the final word in the Russian camp of the young. All this coincided with certain special influences that played on the literary mind towards the close of the war, Mark Twain's *The Mysterious Stranger*, for instance, published in 1916, and Adams's *Education*, two years later. Mark Twain had seen life as meaningless and Adams predisposed the young to feel that democracy in America was a failure, while the return of the expatriates from Paris, drifting back one by one, bred still more furious outcries of comparison and censure. Those who had lived in the most beautiful of cities, with so much that pleased the sensual man, together with so much exposed surface of the human, were convinced that the ugly town was an American invention, and they saw everywhere spiritual poverty, intellectual anæmia, universities that looked like shoe factories and a cowardly press.

Repatriated, in other words, the expatriates on the whole agreed with the "Thirty Against America" who had remained at home,—a phrase of the old novelist Henry B. Fuller for the short-lived assemblage of minds from which had sprung *Civili-*

*zation in the United States.* For, while these were by no means condemnatory merely, or of one mood or point of view, they were inclined to accept the belief of Robert Herrick, Fuller's friend, that ours was the "least lovely" of civilizations. Just before what Harold Stearns later described as his "flight from reality," he had proposed to me, then to Lewis Mumford and finally to Spingarn, Mencken, Ring Lardner and others, a critical survey of American life in virtually every aspect, sport, science, philosophy, poetry, painting and so on. Stearns, who had been living in Greenwich Village since he had left Harvard, where his chosen teacher had been Santayana, was a quintessential Villager who had edited the old fortnightly *Dial* and haunted the Liberal Club and Boni's bookshop. First or last, he had fallen in with most of the writers he drew into this group, Walter Pach, Conrad Aiken, Robert Morss Lovett, —along with those whom I have already mentioned,—Hendrik van Loon, who was living in the Village, Frank Moore Colby, the essayist, Deems Taylor, Elsie Clews Parsons and George Jean Nathan. Another was John Macy, who had married the teacher of Helen Keller and with whom I worked for some months on *The Freeman,* one of the precursors of the critical movement of the twenties. Among the others were Ernest Boyd, who wrote *As an Irishman Sees It,* and Henry Longan Stuart, our Westport friend.

There were few actual meetings of these rebel intellectuals, so called, who were at the same time both bitter and hopeful and who felt that things American were almost always wrong but that there were usually cures for the unlovely and the evil. They were against a social life that seemed emotionally and aesthetically starved as well as against "reaction," the common foe,—the quality and spirit of a business civilization,—against "efficiency," "pecuniary standards" and those who, as Sinclair

Lewis said, made Patrick Henry orations about windshield-wipers. They disliked "Americanitis," the disease of high tension, and they were inclined on the whole to feel with Theodore Dreiser that America was the land of Bottom the Weaver. No doubt they were rather more aware of what they were against than of what they were for; and they were sometimes inaccurate and ignorant, as Bernard De Voto remarked when the climate of opinion changed a few years later. Then it seemed scarcely credible that, as Harold Stearns said, it was next to impossible to get anyone to write about religion. No one could be induced to grapple with a subject that was to become in time almost an obsession.

Perhaps the general negativism of which these essays were a type had certain harmful effects on the coming generation, destroying all confidence in a country that was, after all, the writers' own but that came to be regarded, so often, with scorn. Separated as most of the essayists were from any strong sense of the popular life, they seemed to have little affection for the world they lived in, and some of them showed the Dadaistic influence and the spirit of contempt and futility to which this gave birth. They criticized America by comparing it with Europe, which it never occurred to them to criticize at all, differing in this from Emerson who, having Asia always in mind, surveyed from a great height all the Western cultures. Perhaps it was childish not to see many of the faults of America as a natural result of the feverish growth of the country, along with the immigration that Waldo Frank described as a "chaos of dissolved ethnic cultures." But this undertaking was part of the movement of national self-examination that was involved in our general coming-of-age, while the constant discussion of literary problems made American literature, for the first time, seem really important. In earlier days both Whitman and

Howells had vainly tried to make it so, but too many influences in the country had pointed back to Europe.

Always a symbol, Harold Stearns was more than ever one when he "re-affirmed" America in still another book, reappearing as "a ghost of a generation that has gone" who had found that "after all, a real world exists here." That was at a time when, as Albert Nock said, the trouble in Europe turned one's thoughts "with something almost like tolerance" to this country. With the rise of the Nazi-Fascists, this reversal of feeling was characteristic of many a censorious mind of earlier days, for, with all its abuses, our prosaic republic seemed curiously inculpable beside Mussolini's Italy or Germany or Spain. When had it ever seen anything like the venomous tribal race-hatreds of Europe or the governmental hooliganism or the wholesale bestialities that marked these great civilized nations we admired so much? But that was in the thirties when George Grosz, the painter, coming to New York, found there a "healthier, freer, happier" world than anything he had known in the boiling caldron, the Europe, with its heavy air of oncoming events, he described in *A Little Yes and a Big No*. In the twenties there were few young Americans, few, at least, whom I knew, who felt as many were to feel a decade later.

## CHAPTER XII

# MY BOOKS

D URING THESE years I was possessed by the notion that American writers were, for whatever reasons, foredoomed to fail, a notion that others shared no doubt and that was taken up later by the novelists Ernest Hemingway and Scott Fitzgerald. For when Fitzgerald said, "There are no second acts in American lives," he was repeating in other words Hemingway's remark, "Something happens to our good writers at a certain age. We destroy them in many ways." What was this "something" that happened and how could one explain the obvious miscarriage of many American talents, so that our literature seemed to me, in the phrase of D. H. Lawrence, "a disarray of falling stars coming to naught"? Since the high days of New England only a handful of writers had fully coined the metal in themselves, as Hawthorne and Emerson had done, Thoreau and Parkman, while countless others had failed to grow for want of self-knowledge, perhaps, or was it some lack in the native soil and air? Our literary world was a kind of limbo, as it seemed to me, where the wraiths of writers were blown hither and thither, abortive or, like Henry Adams and so many others, neglected, and often developing in strange and monstrous ways.

I had long been full of this idea when I wrote *The Ordeal*

*of Mark Twain* at Carmel in 1918 and 1919; and the theme was discussed for several years by others who saw that our writers were constantly breaking down or cracking up. They "sold out" or they fizzled out "after looking gigantic at first," as John Hyde Preston was to put it, when they reached early middle age and the light seemed to go out in them and they fell into ruts and formulas or ceased to write. As Mrs. Lightfoot Lee had said in Adams's *Democracy*, they grew six inches high and then they stopped, and even in our more vital time when literary talent abounded we were to see this happen often enough. Was not *The Crack-Up* soon to show how Scott Fitzgerald lost his way, aware that he had not fulfilled his promise?—and there was Sherwood Anderson, who missed the target so many times, producing, after all, so few successes. He knew he had entered too many blind alleys, neglecting his proper gift, following false leads, distracted from his main purpose, knowing himself so little as to think that he could write plays while he was haunted by thoughts of artistic failure. Something like this, it seemed to me, was, with American writers, rather more the rule than the exception,—as one looked back from about 1920,—and I wondered how far one could blame for this the famous provincial conditions that Henry James had bewailed in the story of his youth. How far had they been "visibly killed by the lack of air to breathe," as Santayana said of the young poets who had been his friends? In point of self-knowledge, in any case, and the power of self-development, our writers could seldom compare with the writers of England, who knew so well what they were fitted to do and how to go about it and were able to make so much more of themselves and their gifts. Because of this difference we had few indeed to set beside Shaw, Wells, W. H. Hudson, Kipling, Bennett, Chesterton, George Moore or Yeats.

I was all the more concerned with this because the writer seemed to me so vitally important to society as well as to the reader, full as I was of the ideas not only of Emerson and Whitman but of many of the great modern European writers. For ever since I had turned away from the history of art to literature I had been a voracious reader of the "lives of the poets,"—to use the word in its Crocean sense. I read them as eagerly as a monk reads the lives of the saints,—"to become used to good models," as Nietzsche put it,—and Tolstoy, Chekhov, Dostoievsky, Flaubert and many another confirmed my serious notion of the writer's role. Like Ibsen, for whom literature had its redemptive aspect, Leopardi said that "in literature alone the regeneration of our country can have a substantial beginning," and I had conceived a sort of composite mental picture of the great writer as he might and should be. I thought of him as one who made the fullest use of his own powers and added a new dimension to the world about him; for to me the great writer was not only the voice of his people and his time but one who, in Berenson's phrase, enhanced their life. This implied an organic relation between the writer and his world, and it also implied that if he was to "regenerate" or "redeem" this world he must impose upon it his own values. To accept the values of his world, to adapt himself to his environment, would be to fall short of the model in a fatal fashion, and one would fall short equally if one lost touch with one's natural world, for, that being so, how could one work upon it?

Of course, I am rationalizing here the inner logic of a case that I saw only emotionally during these years, and I do not remember at what point I saw it in these terms, although for a good part of a decade it really obsessed me. It was the case that embodied itself in a biographical trilogy,—two "cautionary" studies and one "exemplary" study,—after my "thesis" in *Mark Twain,* and my "antithesis" in *Henry James,* led, in a *Life of Emerson,* to the "synthesis" of Hegel. In this last I hoped to produce the image of a literary model, a whole and central figure, in American terms, an aim in which I was predestined to fail if only because Emerson's world was too remote from the modern American scene. In this threefold portrait, as it were, of the writer in America I meant to touch all the main aspects of our literary life, its characteristic problems and the typical ways in which it failed, together with the true nature of the writer's success. The work throughout was intended to be emblematic, but I was obliged to feel in the end how partial had been my own success in attempting to canvass in this way so multiform a subject. Regarding the problems of our literary life, Emerson had been resourceful and wise beyond any other American of the present or the past, for no other had thrown so much light on the natural history of the writer and the art of conserving, developing and expending his powers. This was a subject about which I never ceased to think, and as, year after year, I saw our writers stumbling about in the dark, failing in the same old ways or giving up the fight, I wondered why American critics remained so incurious about it, indifferent as they seemed to everything but technical questions.

My *Life of Emerson* was a sort of imputed autobiography, written to a large extent in Emerson's own words, while the other two were psychoanalytic, more or less, and consequently bound to result in distortion. For this method reduces a person to a type, a congeries of inhibitions, complexes and what not, in place of the individual in his concrete fullness, and, in *The Ordeal of Mark Twain,* my over-concern with psychology left no room for literary appreciation. Or, for that matter, human appreciation either. Sherwood Anderson, who was bent on "selling" me "Twain," as he put it, feeling that I did not properly understand him, showed me, when the book was published, where I had fallen short,—I should have sung the praises of *Huckleberry Finn*. Many years later, in New York, when we were dining together under a portrait of Mark Twain in a semi-public room, Sherwood, glancing up at this, said, "There was a lovely man,"—and that was indeed one way of looking at him. He was perhaps more centrally the champion of justice, the hater of shams and the generous lovable genius than the man I had pictured, as Mark Twain's humour had a positive value that I had all but entirely failed to suggest. Then, if he was money-mad, so was Balzac; and how could one speak of failure in connection with a writer who was the most successful of his time, if only because he had written one great book? Later, when I studied Mark Twain again for my literary history, I was to see all these objections clearly, yet I still felt he had made the great refusal and that *The Ordeal of Mark Twain* was substantially just. I remembered how I had put it together as one puts together a picture-puzzle in which every fragment has its inevitable place, and I had not consciously invented the picture,—it sprang for me out of the evidence with almost the natural force of a revelation. I did not see how one could shake the logic of the book.

What was I presenting? Perhaps only half of the real Mark Twain but certainly much, if not the whole, of a well-known abstract character, the typical American author as we knew him at the moment. Sinclair Lewis suggested that I should write another book applying to living authors the verdict of this one. Mentioning names we all knew, he wished me to show how certain talents, apparent at the outset, turned into "dreary machines," whether because of some magazine policy, money or good-fellow friends, or "general Americanitis,"—what was the reason? All American writers knew the pressures of a business civilization, almost all had been urged to go into business, and I had stated the obvious fact that they could not conform to such a world if they were to open new horizons for it. Yet they seemed eager to conform, they did not wish to be "different," and, as if to make amends for the difference they could not escape, they often pretended that they were in business. Or, ashamed of being writers, they gave themselves out in Jack London's way as proprietors of hygienic pigsties or prosperous farmers. Jack London himself had written to Waldo Frank at *The Seven Arts,* saying that if such a magazine had existed twenty years before he would not have turned out his "pap of pretty lies." At authors' dinners I had watched the heavy-jowled nabobs of our magazine world gazing at some visiting writer from across the ocean, some spare, withdrawn soul who had lived perhaps on bread and cheese while he had kept the zest for spiritual adventure. How humble one could see they felt before that image of contemptuous pride, that emblem of literary power. No doubt the chief reason for their failure to grow was that, in this country, the literary tradition was not clear or strong, so that they were never properly aware of the vocation in which the writer finds his real rewards.

So much for the question of "adaptation." The main alternative had always been flight, and this fact had given birth to "the classic debate of American culture, Should an American artist stay at home?" (I am quoting Waldo Frank's *In the American Jungle.*) This I had set out to study in the case of Henry James, the greatest of all the American expatriates or exiles. It seemed to me obvious that "something went wrong with his development," as one of his English admirers, F. R. Leavis, was to observe in time in *The Great Tradition.* Following somewhat the same line that I had taken years before, this critic rejected as "bad" or "not successful" the three long later novels of Henry James, *The Ambassadors*, *The Golden Bowl* and *The Wings of the Dove*, adding that the famous Prefaces were "not merely difficult but unrewarding," while he took one back to this writer's "happiest" phase. He described *The Bostonians* and *The Portrait of a Lady* as "the two most brilliant novels in the language," saying that, with them and with *Washington Square* and other novels of their time, James's genius functioned at its "freest and fullest." Then what Dr. Leavis called the "hypertrophy of technique" set in and we had the indirections and subtleties of James's decline.

This was precisely what I had said in *The Pilgrimage of Henry James*, although, as it happened, Dr. Leavis, agreeing with my verdict, disagreed with my explanation of it. Yet it seemed to me equally obvious that James, as his brother William said, had lost touch with the "vital facts of human character," and this was because he had lost touch with the people whom he understood, his fellow-Americans either at home or in Europe. In short, he had "forfeited" the "precious advantage in ceasing to tread his native soil" that James imputed to Hawthorne just at the moment when he also said of Turgenev, regarding this matter of the "native soil," that "all great novelists savour strongly of it." He had also said it was dangerous for a novelist "to project himself into an atmosphere in which he has not a transmitted and inherited property"; and was it not evident that he himself failed to assimilate as a novelist should the English world that he had set out to conquer? Why, otherwise, after a few attempts to write as an English novelist, did he revert to the abandoned American themes, to the "international subject" that had long since "faded" from his mind, as he had said so emphatically years before?

Of course, all this was to mean little to the critics of a later time for whom indirectness and "difficulty" were positive values, who cared nothing for "character," the "air of reality" or the "solidity of specification" that James himself had called the "supreme virtues" of fiction. They loved his "crooked corridors" in the face of Tolstoy, who wished to get "at once down to business" when he began the greatest of the world's novels, and they were not dissatisfied with James's ghost-like presences floating in a void, shadow-like passionless women and fish-blooded men. It meant little to them that his later fictions were like cobwebs, as Somerset Maugham remarked, "which at any moment the housemaid's broom with brutal common sense may sweep away," for the formalist critics, unconcerned with literature in its relation to life, cared for problems of texture and structure only. But as, more and more, with the passing of time, they dominated the critical world, I questioned, as Whitman had done, these "professional elects," feeling that people of ripe heart and mind who know the world as they know life are always the ultimate judges of the value of novels. (In that sense, Sir Desmond MacCarthy was undoubtedly right when he said, "The public is the critic.") As I knew these people, they usually agreed with William James, who wrote to his brother that "the *core* of literature is solid," and who remarked to another correspondent, "I for one am no longer able to read a word that he [Henry] writes." Yet who was more interested than William James in every phase of real life and in every novel that gave one a feeling for it? He was not a Philistine, as the lovers of Henry James implied when they were obliged to face this condemnation.

So I might have felt sure that I was right in the general estimate of James's work that Dr. Leavis confirmed a few years later, and it struck me as an interesting fact that five novelists wrote to me to say that they agreed with my conclusions. They were all writers of integrity of the older generation who had attempted themselves to novelize the country and who might have been supposed to wish that Henry James had failed when he himself gave up the attempt to do so. But I do not think this was the motive that turned them against his later work, as John Jay Chapman rejected James altogether, saying, "I am so out of sympathy with his temperament that I have never read him, but I read your book . . . muttering all the time that the vaporous subject was not worth" the treatment, "yet feeling it was all true." What Chapman called James's vaporousness was the general objection, and to Ellen Glasgow, who had met him in London several times, James, so unlike Hardy, "seemed to ring hollow." It shocked Robert Herrick, for the rest, that James denatured his early work when he re-wrote the conversations in it, when his Christopher Newmans and Longmores ceased to be their American selves and gen-erally spoke in the later Jamesian manner. Aside from this, Herrick was repelled by the "pathetic provincialism" of Henry James's relation to the world he had adopted. He had cor-rected this young man for addressing him as "Mr. James," say-ing, "Only butlers do that, my dear Herrick."

With so much corroboration, my mind should have been at rest, I should have felt that for me the case was settled, espe-cially when so many others felt as I did, when, for one, AE, challenging James's false air of profundity, said that he "made intricacies in the shallows." Then there was Paul Elmer More, who, praising Anthony Trollope, spoke of the "endless chatter" of the later Henry James, together with his "tangled sleave of oblique suggestions,"—all of which justified my regret that James had been taken as a model by many beginning novelists in this country. For was he not inevitably sterilizing as an in-

fluence on others? He warned them away from more congru-
ous models like Tolstoy or Dostoievsky, whom he called "baggy
monsters" or "mere fluid puddings," and, imposing upon them
his own "right" form, he kept them from finding their own
form, which ought to have sprung out of their subject-matter.
Moreover, he induced in them a kind of literary opiumism in
which the realities of character ceased to matter and life and
love were felt to be somehow vulgar.

So I was convinced most of the time, but,—to continue with
my doubts,—was this all really due to expatriation, evident as
it so often was that the American emigré seemed to lose in
Europe his natural bearings? There was Edith Wharton whose
work deteriorated more and more after she had "cut her roots,"
in the phrase of Percy Lubbock, as if to prove that the American mind could not maintain its integrity abroad, that it was
all but inevitably compromised in Europe. Why else did Henry
James himself say so often to American friends that he should
not have lost touch with his countrypeople, and was it not
the moral of his life of Story that American artists might better
stay at home? Both James and Edith Wharton were perpetu-
ally troubled by a sense that their literary lives might have
been built on a mistake, that perhaps Dostoievsky was right
for them when he said, "A writer should not leave his country
for too long a time. He should live one life with her. Otherwise he is lost." But I had set out to make a case and I could
not be sure of it, for there were other possible explanations of
James's anomalous development or failure to develop, and I
was "harried with doubts," as Arnold Bennett said he was
when he too attacked James's later novels. For him *The Golden
Bowl* was an "arid desert." Was I insensitive, was I blind to
an obvious greatness? I felt that for nothing in the world
would I ever open again any of Henry James's later novels and

that his appearance of depth was wholly an illusion; and yet regarding all this I fell into a state of irresolution that actually became for me a virulent illness. Along with one or two other circumstances, it carried me into a formidable nervous breakdown.

Nor was I encouraged later to feel that I was right when James became one of the idols of a long generation, when the new critics defended his last phase as the major phase and no university was complete without a "Henry James expert." The new climate of opinion in literature, largely created in Paris, had been created wholly by expatriated persons, Pound, Eliot, Gertrude Stein, Joyce, Ford and Lawrence, exiles from their respective countries who could not feel that literature had any vital connection with "native lands." The writer for them was above localities and countries, and, moreover, they were not greatly interested in character as such or the "old-fashioned human element," as D. H. Lawrence called it. People were apt to seem to them as they seemed to Wyndham Lewis, "rather walking notions than 'real' entities," and so there was nothing amiss for them in the later Henry James with his "No. 1" and "No. 2" young men. Meanwhile, when questions of technique filled the minds of critics, he had much of technical interest for them, at a time, moreover, when the religion of art had become virtually the only religion. With the "divine principle" of his work, the "sacred years" that he had known and his "celestial, soothing, sanctifying process," James surrounded himself with an aura of priesthood.

For the rest, with the new generation, the old question of colonialism had gone by the board, and so had the other old question of expatriation. They had ceased to have any meaning for the younger writers, while I myself had been involved in both; and I was to realize, looking back, that I had been quarrelling with myself when I appeared to be quarrelling with Henry James. For, like many of my friends, I too had been enchanted with Europe, and I had vaguely hoped to continue to live there. It struck me that if I was always "straining to read the face of America,"—Paul Rosenfeld's phrase for my obsession,—it was because of an over-determination, and perhaps the question of expatriation had so possessed my mind because this mind itself had been divided. Only my reason had told me what I later came to feel, that the French aphorist Doudon was right when he said, "One must live, struggle and die among one's own." I mean he was right for those who were organized as I was.

In the end the question of Henry James resolved itself for me in a certain general notion of literary values,—that there is a gulf in judgment and feeling between those who see literature in terms of itself and those who see it in terms of a wider connection. In this respect and regarding James, I stood in the second category with AE, Maugham, More, Bennett and an army of others, minds as diverse as they well could be yet all agreeing that substance and depth are indispensable elements of a great novel. They might have agreed that James was a fine literary artist without ceasing to feel that his later work was poor indeed in qualities that are still more important than literary art. Was it not irrelevant to ask, as James asked of Tolstoy and Dostoievsky, "What do they artistically mean?"— for, baggy monsters that they were, along with Dickens, in James's mind, they were no less than supreme as both novelists and writers. And as so many novelists of our own twenties lost their substance and grasp of life, it struck me that the case of James was really a symbol,—I mean those novelists who had grown up in the so-called expatriate religion of art with a feeling that native lands are not important. Judging by these later cases, it seemed to me disastrous for the novelist to lose his natural connection with an inherited world that is deeply his own, when, ceasing to be "in the pedigree" of his own country, he is no longer an expression of the communal life.

## CHAPTER XIII

# A SEASON IN HELL

"TIMES HAVE always been like these. We were born in an off period, 1880-1914, and we can fool ourselves into believing that that was a 'normal era.' It was not. It was a short and pleasant breathing space. Now we are experiencing normal times." So, in 1938, Hendrik van Loon wrote to me, long after the decade I have been recollecting, when there had been a total change in the climate of opinion and feeling that sways the minds of writers and colours their books. In 1920, in the United States, Utopia had still seemed at hand, as it seemed also in Russia after 1917, although it was a lost cause in the rest of Europe, while the ideas of the Enlightenment were active still in American minds and in the minds especially of American writers. But the time had come when these ideas, as a younger writer was to say, "evoke our doubt or mistrust" and "cause us anguish." I am sure that in these words Jacques Barzun was expressing a widespread point of view of the new generation.

Many have attempted to define the change from the "infrared" epoch of the past to the "ultra-violet" epoch of the thirties and after,—to follow Arthur Koestler's diagnosis,—when humanity seemed to pass into a dark night of the soul. Nothing could have been more marked than the transformation of the literary world from the state of mind of a dozen years before when, as Waldo Frank had said, at the time of *The Seven Arts,* "There is a murmur of suppressed excitement in the air." It was, he added, "like that which hovers over a silent crowd before the appearance of a great procession." Had this procession come and gone? Certainly no one in 1930 looked for any such thing to appear in the future, for "a dreadful apathy, unsureness and discouragement is felt to have fallen upon us," Edmund Wilson wrote in the following year. Gertrude Stein said, in fact, that there was no future,—there was "no future any more"; while Paul Rosenfeld, editing *The American Caravan,* noted that after 1930 every contribution to this yearbook was tragic. In the great number of papers that were submitted to it, he said, there was not one cheerful composition. Paul was dismayed by this uniform note, so different from that of the time when he, like all our contemporaries, had begun to write and when he had half expected to see "ideas at every street corner and rivers of living water in the street." Over the gate of the thirties one seemed to see the words, "Abandon hope, all ye who enter here."

The writers were generally prepared at least to abandon all interest in the future of the world unless they were Marxists who did not believe in the will and who thought that Utopia was coming by an automatic process; while a series of anti-Utopias in the years to come were to present the future as inevitably dismal. Feeling that they could do nothing whatever to change this unpromising picture, the writers quite naturally looked in the other direction and many began to idealize the Middle Ages that fixed the mind on another world and life. Nor were they more disposed to contemplate the future when the menace of atomic destruction rose over the world and when, like old men who fear that tomorrow they are going to

develop some fatal disease, they buried all thoughts of the future in thoughts of the past. Constantly more insecure, they
were obsessed with security and the orthodoxy that gave them
a feeling of this, and, in their dream of authority and unity,
they seemed to wish to avoid the paths that had led to so many
developments of the livelier twenties. Adventurousness, curi-
osity and independence had lost their charm in a world that
was full of snares and pitfalls, and they were inclined to share
Cardinal Newman's "fierce thoughts against the Liberals" whose
gullibility, they felt, had deceived and betrayed them. Nor
could they continue to trust themselves when all humanity, as
it seemed to them, had revealed such fathomless depths of
depravity and evil.

For, with the new generation, the moral effects of the first
world war spread to the remotest corner of the realm of writers,
and this reproduced the symptoms of the Hellenistic age, as we
have been taught by eminent scholars to see it. The sense of
failure in that age, the loss of hope in the present world and
in organized effort and human calculation, together with the
lapse of self-confidence that accompanied this, had developed
in the Greeks too a pessimistic mysticism that was focussed on
a dream-world far away. Humanism, as the thirties advanced,
became more and more a byword, and art, as Ortega said, was
dehumanized also, while the mind of the present ransacked
the past for earlier minds, both small and great, that confirmed
its own disillusion and despair.

*

*       *

Meanwhile, I experienced my own season in hell.

One day during these later years of which I have been writing I happened to visit a certain refugee author, an Austrian,

known the world over, with only a few months to live, who had settled in a college town not far away. I found him in a cluttered shabby room in a dreary students' lodging-house, looking out on a back yard full of mud and rubbish, where a closet door stood open revealing his wardrobe, a battered old hat and a threadbare coat or two. In one corner was a kerosene stove on which he evidently cooked the meals that he drew from bottles and cans piled beside it, and various noxious smells and sounds drifted, as the talk went on, through the dingy golden-oak woodwork of the windows and the walls. He remarked that he was sixty-five and it struck me how easy it would be to take all this for granted if one were twenty,—when anything will pass for picturesqueness,—while many another at his age, obliged to exist in a similar way, would have hanged themselves forthwith from the door of the closet. But he was obviously living in quite another world. Apropos of nothing, he suddenly exclaimed, "The Engadine is beautiful. It is really beautiful! I know because I have just been rereading the novel I wrote about it fifteen years ago."

This great man was living in a dream of his own imagination, and all writers, in fact, exist under a sort of spell or, one might say, within a magic circle. They live under a dome of many-coloured glass, and they see the world, including themselves, as this many-coloured glass iridescently stains it. If the dome is broken, if the bubble bursts, as one might otherwise put it, and they see life in its nakedness, or see themselves so,—as mere old men in sordid lodging-houses,—they are apt to fall into the melancholy leading to despair which the monks called acedia in the Middle Ages. Most of the recorded instances of mediæval suicide were occasioned by acedia in the monasteries, I have been told, and something similar surely accounts for the catastrophic endings that have so often marked the lives of writers.

There came a time in the middle twenties when my own bubble burst, when the dome under which I had lived crumbled into ruin, when I was consumed with a sense of failure, a feeling that my work had all gone wrong and that I was mistaken in all I had said or thought. What had I been doing? I had only ploughed the sea, as a certain great man once remarked, and I thought of my writing "with rage and shame," E. M. Forster's phrase for his own feeling about his early work. I was pursued especially with nightmares in which Henry James turned great luminous menacing eyes upon me. I was half aware, in connection with him, of the division within myself, and with all the bad conscience of a criminal I felt I had viewed him with something of Plato's "hard little eye of detraction." In short, in this middle of my life, I was thoroughly bedevilled. I saw myself as a capsized ship at night with the passengers drowned underneath and the keel in the air. I could no longer sleep, I scarcely sat down for a year, I lived in a Plutonian psychical twilight. Even the sun was off-colour to me, I was a prey to vertigo, at moments my brain seemed to be deranged, and when I napped for an hour or so I dreamed that I was about to be hanged or that something had occurred in my blood-stream that was evidently fatal. All my affections and interests fell into abeyance, and it seemed to me that, where normal depressions occasionally sank to zero, mine sank from zero indefinitely down. The nadir of common depressions was the peak of mine. Nine-tenths of all my energy was involved in a neurosis and barely one-tenth was left for living.

I had always been possessed by this idea or that, usually the notion of the book I happened to be writing, which I pursued like a beagle with his nose to the ground; and I was possessed now with a fantasy of suicide that filled my mind as the full moon fills the sky. It was a fixed idea. I could not expel this fantasy that shimmered in my brain, and I saw every knife as something with which to cut one's throat and every high building as something to jump from. A belt was a garotte for me, a rope existed to hang oneself with, the top of a door was merely a bracket for the rope, every rusty musket had its predestined use for me and every tomb in a graveyard was a place to starve in. I could see an axe only as lethal and every bottle meant for me something to be swallowed in splinters or to slash one's wrists with, while even the winter snow fell in order to give one pneumonia if one spent a night lying on the ground. Meanwhile, every morning, when I began to sleep again, I awoke with my arms folded over my breast. I had been dreaming that I was dead at last and unconsciously arranged my limbs in the posture of a mummy.

In my *crise à quarante ans* I shrank from all human relations, and this explained the image Paul Rosenfeld happened upon in the fine essay he wrote about me. He spoke of a house with the shades drawn and a man sitting within, a man who could not hear the knock when life drove up to the door with her merry summons. How could Paul ever have guessed what was happening in that house? Nor did Sherwood Anderson know why it was that we drifted apart when he wrote, "I did not put Brooks aside. He put me aside." But, calling me a New Englander, though he knew well I was not one, he pictured in a striking phrase my mental condition. Observing that I had the "beauty" of the New England mind, he said I suffered from its "cold inner fright."

One of the doctors whom I saw and who had read *The Ordeal of Mark Twain* asked me if I considered that "reason" or "emotion" had been the determining element in my mind and work. The question had never occurred to me, but, recalling my struggles to make this book logical and clear, I replied, "Reason, I suppose," and the doctor smiled. He shook his head and walked away, and I saw at once that he was right. I had always worked by following my nose, I had never been able to think anything out but rather *felt* things out in a cumbersome fashion, and, writing always intuitively, I was emotionally paralyzed now or, as Dr. Brill said, "too disturbed for treatment." My wife had written to Dr. Jung, whom Joel Spingarn knew well and who replied sympathetically and kindly from Zurich. The psychology of my illness, he wrote, was transparent enough: what I had was "chronic melancholia" and "a terribly hard case for treatment, if possible at all." He added, "Things seem to have gone very far," saying that even to attempt a cure would be hazardous under the circumstances. He then suggested the old expedient of a year on a Western ranch, for, in primitive surroundings, complicated situations often dissolved, as he put it, or were eased at least.

The upshot was that, like Peer Gynt, I went back to the button-moulder. I was to spend four years in houses of the dead, or, as one might say, the wounded, or the about-to-be-reborn, at Stockbridge, at Katonah, at White Plains and in England. It struck me at once that my fellow-inmates all had queer eyes, which I took for a sign of the clan I now belonged to, the clan of those to whom they said, "What *were* you?" as if you had actually arrived in the land of shades. All I remember of Stockbridge now was a drive one day to Pittsfield and Herman Melville's farm on a lonely road, where one still saw the name "Arrowhead" boldly carved on the carriage-block and a house all in sagging disrepair. It was a dirtyish yellow and some windows were broken. But there was the big chimney of which Melville had written and the famous piazza he had built, to remind himself in the country of the deck of a ship, with its straw-coloured planks rotting away. Peeping through the boards that covered the windows, I saw some of his old folios within, together with a big ship's model on a bracket on the wall, which took me seventy years back to the day when this *exalté* had also undergone a season in hell.

I was to find myself presently in an English sanitarium where I spent eight months at Harrow-on-the-Hill in a long low Queen Anne manor-house that was later to become the infirmary of the neighbouring Harrow school. There I conceived the delusion that I was about to be buried alive, not in the earth but walled in a small chamber; and I believed that "they" were coming for me. For many mornings, waking early from an artificial sleep, I heard them putting together a large box for me below, a box that, in my fantasy, had arrived in sections to be hammered together in the house with nails or pegs. To me this accounted for the resonant clatter of the housemaids who were merely pulling up the Venetian blinds. If I was not to be buried alive why should people have talked to me about the crypt of St. Paul's or the wax funeral figures,— the Effigies,—in their glass cases in Westminster Abbey? I was persuaded that the doctor had induced Parliament to pass a bill enabling him to bury me alive, a notion that later suggested to me how large was the ego in my cosmos (in the phrase of the elderly German in Kipling's tale). There was even a day when I stood by the table in my circular room in the tower,— it was a sunny spring day, the curtains were flapping, and the daffodils were all out in the grass below,—when I had a sudden vision of the end of the world, a catastrophe caused solely by my fate. For this had occasioned a breakdown of all who were attached to me and who were also, in consequence, buried alive, while those who were attached to them came to the same end, and so on, and on, *ad infinitum*. As in some monstrous cosmic general strike, all mankind was engulfed, all movement ceased. I could see the steamships stopping in the middle of the ocean, while invisible waves of horror encircled the world.

There were other trances, like opium dreams, illusions of infinite time and space, into which I fell abruptly during these four years. I remember, at home again, looking up at windows that had meant much to me not long before, and wondering how it was possible for me, in 1929, to have bridged the vast chasm of years since 1906. That year seemed more remote than the great days of Egypt. Meanwhile, I found myself in the rose-embosomed hospital that William Seabrook described in his book *Asylum* where the ornamental iron-work over the windows disguised the actuality of bars. The long corridor was hung with steel-engravings of William Tell, the Parthenon, King Lear and his daughters, and the guards, patrolling the red carpet, kept under constant surveillance the doorless rooms in which anything might happen. A rattling of the main door, at nine o'clock sharp in the morning, proclaimed the official entrance of the froglike doctor, the bearded panjandrum with the long chain of keys and his retinue of assistants, orderlies and nurses. Passing from patient to patient, scattering insults and ironies,—a sort of cold-shock treatment that was then in vogue,—he would order the hydropathic hose for the man who had jumped off Brooklyn Bridge and the pack for the young man who presently drowned himself (when he was permitted to go home for a Sunday). Then, with carpentry, basketry, weaving, one went back to the kindergarten, with the hope, supposedly, that a new man would grow from the little child one had become again.

Out of the purgatorial mist that now envelops the scene for

me more than one tragic and shadowy character emerges. There was the famous doctor who had become a destructive child and who tried to smash his bedstead in the middle of the night. Then there was the old gentleman whom I saw standing on a chair in his room attaching his suspenders to the chandelier, in a patient methodical effort to encircle his neck, and there was the florist whose name was emblazoned on many a New York street, a religious maniac who was also homicidal. He fell to his knees and prayed one day when four of us were playing bridge, then suddenly sprang up and tried to strangle my partner. There was the newspaper publisher who said he must see the doctor at once about an affair involving ten million dollars, whose aeroplane was ticking outside waiting to take him to Africa where he was going for a spell of big-game hunting. He hadn't a minute to spare, he said, then, seizing a large flower-pot, he threw it through the window and sat down on the floor with a wild laugh. There was a charming old man, besides, whom one saw strolling about the grounds in white flannel trousers and a parti-coloured blazer,—General A., I was told he was, and I knew this could not be true because I had read his obituary ten years before. I had read this because he was the uncle of one of my friends and I had met him when I was a boy; but, dead as he was supposed to be, this really was General A., whose family had announced that he was dead when they shut him up. He had even escaped once and appeared at his club in New York, where the attendants who had known him took him for a ghost and whence he had been spirited back to the hospital again. There, I was told, whenever he could, this beautifully groomed old gentleman rubbed in his hair the poached eggs from his breakfast tray. Dreadful to me was the daily exit of the inmates of the so-called violent ward who appeared, in a long queue, for exercise just before noon, marching in single file, with white-coated orderlies flanking them, and winding through the grounds to the cracking of invisible whips. It was a Doré picture, in real life, from the Inferno. The queue was led by a grey-haired giant, an ex-Presbyterian clergyman, who shouted obscenities and oaths as he capered on the path.

Such are my memories of those years when my existence seemed to me a "lost traveller's dream under the hill"; and even after I came back to life and sailed out clear and free I remained conscious at moments of an abyss beside me. I seemed to catch out of the tail of my eye a cold black draughty void, with a feeling that I stood on the brink of it in peril of my reason; but it was only rarely now that I had this glimpse of the *néant,* and in the end my crisis was invaluable for me. I felt as one of my friends felt after he too struck bottom and had "come up more and more ever since," finding his own grave breakdown a "complete purgation." To me he wrote, "I predict you'll find new springs of energy that you had never suspected"; and so, in fact, it proved to be when I returned to love and work with a feeling that my best years still lay before me. Hawthorne had spoken of the dark caverns into which all men must descend if they are to know anything beneath the surface, or what he called the illusive pleasures of existence. It seemed to me now that I understood him, and I wondered if this did not justify the later phase of the world's mind too and the literary mind that reflected its darkness.